THE ART
OF ~~WAR~~
POLICING

2,500 Years of
Sun Tzu's Combat Wisdom
That Can Revolutionize
Law Enforcement

Richard Meure

43-08 162nd Street
Flushing, NY 11358
www.LooseleafLaw.com
800-647-5547

This publication is not intended to replace nor be a substitute for any official procedural material issued by your agency of employment nor other official source. Looseleaf Law Publications, Inc., the author and any associated advisors have made all possible efforts to ensure the accuracy and thoroughness of the information provided herein but accept no liability whatsoever for injury, legal action or other adverse results following the application or adoption of the information contained in this book.

©2020 by Looseleaf Law Publications, Inc. All rights reserved. No part of this book may be reproduced, stored in a retrieval system, or transcribed, in any form or by any means, electronic, mechanical, photocopying, recording, or otherwise, without the prior written permission of the Copyright owner. For such permission, contact Looseleaf Law Publications, Inc., 43-08 162nd Street, Flushing, NY 11358, (800) 647-5547, www.LooseleafLaw.com.

Library of Congress Cataloging-in-Publication Data
Names: Meure, Richard, author. | Sunzi, active 6th century B.C. Sunzi bing fa. English.
Title: The art of policing : 2,500 years of Sun Tzu's combat wisdom that can revolutionize law enforcement / Richard Meure. Description: Flushing, NY : Looseleaf Law Publications, Inc., [2020] |
    Includes complete text of Sun Tzu's On the art of war, translated by Lionel Giles, 1910. | Includes bibliographical references and index. |
    Summary: "Scenario-based, interactive-training situations preparing officers to survive the unexpected like never before; officer safety issues; strategies used in warfare that can be applied to modern law enforcement; principles continue being used in the ongoing fight against terrorism; officers can take things from Sun Tzu and apply them in their day-to-day activities"-- Provided by publisher.
Identifiers: LCCN 2019044808 (print) | LCCN 2019044809 (ebook) | ISBN 9781608852246 (paperback) | ISBN 9781608852253 (adobe pdf)
Subjects: LCSH: Police. | Police training. | Police psychology.
Classification: LCC HV8031 .M48 2020 (print) | LCC HV8031 (ebook) | DDC 363.2/3--dc23
LC record available at https://lccn.loc.gov/2019044808
LC ebook record available at https://lccn.loc.gov/2019044809

Cover by: *Looseleaf Law Publications, Inc.*

TABLE OF CONTENTS

DEDICATION

As a young man, MSG George R Meure (U.S. Army, retired) fought his way through Europe during World War II as a member of the 8th Infantry Division. He was wounded twice, earned a Bronze Star and a Combat Infantryman's Badge. After the war he stayed in the service during the Korean War and then participated in Operation Red Wing in the Pacific where nuclear weapons were tested. He continued to serve his country during the Vietnam War eventually retiring in 1969. In 1966, I came into his life and he spent the remainder of his time teaching me what it meant to have a strong work ethic, to be a decent person and to have a true love for your country. Along with my mother, I could not have asked for a better upbringing. He left us too soon and I owe a great deal of who I am today to my father, so I dedicated this book to you Dad. I miss you.

ACKNOWLEDGMENTS

The majority of the time I worked on this book over the years was spent alone trying to stay awake during midnight shifts or sitting at the rink during my son's 3-hour hockey practices. However, as the worked progressed several people have helped me along the way by providing suggestions, pointing me in the right direction and taking the time to do some proofreading. Their help was greatly appreciated.

These same individuals have also been a big part of my life as beat partners, teammates, fellow instructors and true friends.

Max Bosel, Kevin Dolezal, Nick Perna, Steve Fine, Dan Mulholland, Casey Donovan, Ramiro Perez, Ken Cochran, Gordon Sievert and Reid Lindblom.

And of course, I need to acknowledge the real cornerstone of my life. Without the true love and support of my wife Jennifer and my two sons, Ryan and Jake this project would have never been completed.

Thank you all for being there and remember guys, what happens on the range stays on the range!

ABOUT THE AUTHOR

In 2016, Rick Meure retired from the Redwood City Police Department in Northern California after a 28-year law enforcement career. He spent the majority of his career working patrol with stints as a Juvenile Detective, Community Policing Officer, School Resource Officer and a Field Training Officer. He was also a founding member of his agencies SWAT Team. He spent 18 years on the team serving has an entry team member, assistant team leader and sniper. During his time with the SWAT Team he had collateral duty with a County Wide Counter Terrorism Team specializing in chemical, biological and nuclear threats. Rick became a certified CA POST Firearms Instructor in 1993 and was responsible for the majority of firearms training for his agency to include both tactical teams he belonged to. He also holds instructor certifications in defensive tactics, patrol rifle, HK MP-5, shoot house and survival shooting, to name a few. He has attended numerous shooting schools conducted by notable instructors.

Currently, Rick is a lead firearms instructor for the South Bay Regional Training Consortium in Northern California. He also teaches several other topics at the Academy to include defensive tactics, tactical emergency medical care, active shooter response and wound ballistics

Rick is the owner and lead instructor for Black Knight Training Group which provides firearms and personal defense training. He has studied Krav Maga for over 20 years and holds a Black Belt from Vanguard Krav Maga. He is a certified Krav Maga Instructor.

Prior to becoming a police officer, Rick spent three years in the U.S. Army has a member of the 3rd US INF Regiment, The President's Honor Guard.

INTRODUCTION

The career of law enforcement has never before had as many challenges to overcome for the officer on the street. According to the FBI's annual report of Law Enforcement Officers Killed and Assaulted (LEOKA), there were 66 officers murdered while on duty and 57,180 feloniously assaulted in 2016. There were an additional 53 officers killed on duty in vehicle crashes and training accidents. To survive today's modern world, officers need to be aware of everything from violent gang members, drug traffickers, an influx of parolees and probationers on the streets, juvenile delinquents and the increasing number of emotionally disturbed and mentally unstable persons. On top of that, officers have to deal with the ever-present threat of workplace violence incidents, active school shooters and terrorist attacks.

Very few, if any, police officers will have to deal with all of these situations in a career, but the likelihood of encountering at least one is 100%. Officers need to train and be prepared for all of these incidents in the event they may encounter them.

To better prepare myself to survive my career in law enforcement, I have read and studied with several excellent instructors who taught tactics on how to succeed being a police officer in these current times, all of which have provided me with some valuable insight into the art of survival. In your own search for quality instructors and training, a quick word of caution. Be careful, because there are some resources out there that do not seem to be reality based. These techniques and resources were neither vetted nor street proven, which makes them dangerous.

With the advent of force-on-force training that uses simulated training rounds and the proliferation of interactive force option simulators, officers are now being exposed to realistic lifesaving training. This type of training is one of the best ways to develop a winning mind-set for officers who may encounter an adversary intent on causing harm. These scenario-based, interactive-training situations are preparing officers to survive the unexpected like never before.

When you study the tactics being employed by officers today, there are similarities throughout the variety of styles that can be utilized in almost every situation. Instructors have tried to document these tactics over time, but no one has been successful in cataloging them all. In fact, that task would be impossible.

Also, there is no one perfect tactic that can be used uniformly for everyone in every situation.

When studying officer safety issues throughout my career, I typically came across a source of valuable insight that was quoted over and over again. This source was able to capture basic tactics in terms that were universal and seemed to transcend time and has been used by militaries for centuries to develop strategies in warfare. They are now being used by business professionals to develop strategies for sales, marketing and management. It is time that these tenants be applied to modern law enforcement.

The source of this information comes from a Chinese military advisor named Sun Tzu, who wrote his original book on bamboo strips around the year 500 BC. His advice to the generals of that time is still relevant today and is required reading in most modern military academies.

Sun Tzu's book, *The Art of War*, has been translated several times with slightly varying results. However, the principles remain the same and have been studied by many great military leaders. Napoleon is known to have studied Sun Tzu. General MacArthur and leaders of the Imperial Japanese Army both drew inspiration from the work to do battle against each other. General Vo Nguyen Giap used principles from *The Art of War* to defeat French and American forces in various battles in Vietnam. This brought Sun Tzu to the attention of modern American military leaders. Generals Schwarzkopf and Powell both used several principles from *The Art of War* to defeat the Iraqi Army in the first Gulf War. The same principles continue to be used in our ongoing fight against terrorism.

It is interesting to note that Sun Tzu's principles, whether knowingly or not, have been used throughout ancient and modern warfare, and no one has been able to compile a more concise or better understanding of the conduct of warfare than he did approximately 2,500 years ago.

I've included a complete version of Sun Tzu's work translated from the original Chinese text in 1910 by Lionel Giles at the end of this book. Giles was a researcher, sinologist and a curator at the British Museum. His translation of *The Art of War* is considered one of the most accurate to date and the one I have primarily referenced in this book. Occasionally, I have used translations from other sources simply because they have been easier to read than Giles's version. These translations essentially convey the same meaning as the original Giles's translation but are written in an easier-to-understand format. When reading any version of *The Art of War*, you will not find specific modern tactical advice. You will find abstract observations that can be treated as "thought producers." In his book, *Sun Tzu at Gettysburg*, Bevin Alexander states, "Sun Tzu's maxims are disarming because, once pointed out, they appear to be the obvious, most sensible thing to do."

In this book, I've taken key concepts from *The Art of War* and applied them to modern law enforcement. The concepts can be used in many more circumstances than what I mention here. It is my intention to make this book a true thought producer in the hopes that officers can take things from Sun Tzu and apply them in their day-to-day activities.

Sun Tzu understood the importance of studying the opposition when he stated, ***The art of war is of vital importance to the state. It is a matter of life and death, a road either to safety or to ruin. Hence it is a subject of inquiry which can, on no account, be neglected.*** Sun Tzu's work has lasted the test of time and will still apply for many years to come.

The same importance should be given to the study of officer safety and law enforcement in general because it is beyond a doubt, "of vital importance to the state."

WHO WAS SUN TZU ?

Sun Tzu is believed to have authored one of the most famous books ever written on military strategy. However, historians have debated Sun Tzu's true origins, some even stating that he did not exist at all, and that Sun Tzu is merely a name given to a collection of strategies collected from many authors. However, most agree that in fact he was an actual man and was the sole author of *The Art of War*.

A Chinese historian named Sima Qian, who lived in the second century BC, wrote a biography of Sun Tzu, which serves as the basis of much of our knowledge about him. Sun Tzu is believed to have been born around 544 BC in the ancient Chinese state of Qi. His birth name was Sun Wu. He was not known as Sun Tzu until he authored his famous book. At the time, it was a custom to name a work after its author.

Sun Tzu's family were members of a class of landless aristocrats that traveled the lands as academic scholars. Sun Tzu had other plans for his future and decided to work as a mercenary. At the time, there was plenty of work for him because there was a constant state of war between the seven nation states seeking to control the vast expanse of fertile lands in eastern China.

During Sun Tzu's travels throughout the country he participated in many battles and studied and learned the strategy used by the generals of the time. In 512 BC, Sun Tzu was hired by King Helu from the State of Wu and appointed to be a general. During this time, it is believed that Sun Tzu wrote his famous book on bamboo strips.

Prior to the King of Wu appointing Sun Tzu to a generalship in his army, he asked him for a demonstration of his skills as a commander. King Helu presented Sun Tzu with 180 of his favorite concubines from the palace and asked Sun Tzu to turn them into soldiers able to follow military commands.

Sun Tzu divided the women into two companies and placed one of the King's favorite concubines at the head of each. He issued each one a spear and asked if they knew the difference between front and back, and right and left. The women began to giggle and answered "Yes." He then instructed them to perform a certain move when they heard the sound of the drum beat. For example, when they heard the drumbeat he ordered "eyes front," and he expected them to look straight ahead. When he ordered "left turn," he expected them to turn to their left, and so on.

After Sun Tzu explained the drill to the women they all agreed they understood. Then to the sound of the drum he ordered "right turn." The women all burst into laughter in response to his command.

Sun Tzu then explained to the women in a patient and controlled tone that if the orders were not clear and distinct and the instructions and words of the commander were not clear, the general is to blame. He again repeated his instructions to the women and again they all agreed they understood.

At the sound of the drum he ordered "right turn." He was met with giggles and laughter for a second time.

Sun Tzu then explained to the women assembled before him that if the commands of the general are clear and the soldiers disobey, it is the fault of the officers. Sun Tzu immediately ordered that the two women he had placed in charge of each group be beheaded. The King protested to Sun Tzu that his favorite concubines had been executed. Sun Tzu explained his reasoning to the King and appointed two new leaders for each group.

As you can imagine the girls were no longer giggling and when they heard the sound of the drums and the command that followed they performed all of the drills perfectly. Sun Tzu then sent a message to the King of Wu stating, "Your majesty, the soldiers are now correctly drilled and perfectly disciplined."

Sun Tzu was then granted a generalship within the King of Wu's army. During many battles serving the King of Wu, Sun Tzu proved his strategies were effective, which led to a successful military career. When Sun Tzu became a general, the Kingdom of Wu's military was considered to be a group of semi-barbarians incapable of achieving any sort of military regulation. After Sun Tzu took control of the military they went on to conquer the neighboring state of Chu, which was the most powerful state during that time in Chinese history. After the defeat of Chu there are no other records of Sun Tzu, and it is thought he went into a form of retirement seeking a peaceful life as opposed to one of combat and battles.

There is no exact record of his death, but it is believed he lived until around 496 BC and died in the State of Wu in China. After his death, his work became known throughout the area to include neighboring Japan. *The Art of War* became an important part of the Samurai warrior culture. Sun Tzu's descendant, Sun Bin, also became a famous scholar in the military arts.

Various scholars and translators still debate the true origins of *The Art of War* and Sun Tzu. A complete version of *The Art of War* was unearthed in China in 1972 that dated back to the second century BC. This proves the existence of the book, but not when or by whom the original text was written. According to some, accounts referenced in the book did not occur in Chinese warfare until long after the book was supposed to have been written in the late 500 BCs, which brings into doubt into the true existence of Sun Tzu.

Either way, the book as we know it today deserves to be read and understood by all who wish to have a distinct advantage when dealing with conflict on a small or large scale.

Part One

OFFICER SAFETY AND TACTICS

Chapter 1   Cultivate a Winning Mind-Set

> *When torrential water tosses boulders, it is because of momentum. The energy is similar to a fully drawn crossbow. The momentum of one skilled in war is overwhelming.*
> —Sun Tzu

I was 17 years old when I first joined the military in 1984 and, like most new recruits, quite impressionable. From the minute I started talking with my recruiters to the time I graduated from Advanced Infantry Training, I was subjected to an organized, deliberate and necessary form of mental manipulation. Some would say brainwashing. The result when I left the red clay of Fort Benning was that I thought I could take on the world and survive. Just the kind of attitude a young infantry soldier needs. Little did I know at the time that in reality I knew just enough to get my ass kicked if I was not careful.

Over the years my training, along with real world experience, has caught up to my attitude, and I now know I can better handle myself in any situation. The Army realized long ago how important it is to cultivate a Winning Mind-Set and that fighting is mostly mental. The military did its best to instill a warrior spirit and mind-set in me and my fellow recruits that was based on centuries of combat experience.

I believe Sun Tzu recognized this principle also, which is that properly training a soldier is more than just teaching someone how to handle a weapon and some basic tactics. It is a total package including honing the mental aspects of being a warrior. According to Sun Tzu, once a soldier has mastered both mental and physical preparations, ***The momentum of one skilled in war is overwhelming.***

You can attend all the training courses, read all the books and watch all the videos available on officer safety, firearms and defensive tactics you want, but if you do not develop the proper mind-set to go along with all of the training, you will be less effective when encountering threats.

You need to take the training you receive and combine it with practical experience. This helps to develop your self-confidence so you can apply your skills successfully. If you do not have confidence, both physically and mentally, to hit the streets and face the dangers out there, you will not succeed.

There are some simple things you can do to help you hone your mental survival skills once you have learned the physical skills. It all starts with a commitment to get better. The late Col. Jeff Cooper, who was the founder of the Gunsite Firearms Training Center and developed the Modern Handgun Fighting system, reminds us that, "Man fights with his mind. His hands and his weapons are simply extensions of his will." Once we understand this, we are on our way to developing a winning mind-set.

By realizing our survival is based mostly on mental preparation there are several techniques we need to practice, to include some self-talk to help prepare ourselves to succeed. We cannot have any self-doubt about our ability to win and prevail in a true life-threatening situation.

As law enforcement officers, we need to develop a mind-set that can become combat oriented in a moment's notice. This is a mind-set that is something we are not all born with. Most humans do not naturally possess an instinctive fighting spirit. It is something that needs to be developed and honed.

We start developing this mind-set when we are young and compete in games, competitions and play sports. When we played, we played for a reason and that was to win. Remember parents who told their kids when they were growing up, "Don't worry about winning. It is all about having fun." Those were for the kids who lost. We cannot think or train like that because the stakes are too high. No one likes to lose but someone has too. The more you prepare and practice before competition, the more likely you will win and make the other guy lose. There will always be someone better than you out there. Your preparation should be aimed at beating that guy.

To start developing a winning mind-set, try this: The next time you are at range training, set up some simple competitions with other officers. A metal dueling tree is an excellent and fun tool to train with when you want to compete against another shooter. You can also try to incorporate some type of sparring in your defensive tactics training.

These two simple activities will greatly enhance the development of your winning mind-set. Remember, whenever you pull the trigger, shoot with a purpose. Even at training think how that paper target or bullseye is trying to kill you. However, remember that police work is not a game. It is life and death and there is no second place. Train that way.

Most people are passive by nature, and they are only occasionally provoked to fight. Only very few of these people will actually engage in a physical confrontation or take up arms. Instead, they will look for help by calling 9-1-1. Others, without provocation, are more aggressive and violent by nature and usually become the criminals of our society, taking out their aggressions on the weak. Then there are those who can channel their aggressive nature for good and become society's protectors.

Lt. Col. Grossman, a former West Point psychology professor and Army Ranger who authored the books *On Killing* and *On Combat*, breaks society down into three categories that may seem simplistic initially, but they are quite accurate in their definition.

The first group that I want to mention live their lives passively. They are the ones who abhor violence and are usually productive members of society. They live protected, sheltered lives and are generally not aware of the dangers of the world. Even if they are, they would deny the possibility of evil things ever occurring to them. When made aware of the possibility of danger, they may still choose to ignore that possibility, believing nothing bad will happen to them. They do not take the time to properly prepare themselves to face reality. These are the people Lt. Col. Grossman refers to as "sheep."

The second category consists of the criminals of our society. Lt. Col. Grossman refers to these guys as "the Wolves." The wolves are the ones that prey on the "sheep." They take advantage of the Sheep's unwillingness and their lack of preparedness to face the harsh reality that evil and danger exist in this world. It is important to remember that the moment you forget that there are evil people willing to do you harm, you will find yourself at the mercy of the Wolves. At that point you simply become part of a flock of Sheep.

The third and final category are the protectors of our society. These are the men and women who have the ability to employ violence when needed morally and legally. They also have a deep appreciation for what is good and right in our society. We call these protectors "Sheep Dogs." The Sheep Dogs are our warriors. They are the select few who will place themselves between the Sheep and the Wolves. The ones who will fight and sometimes lay down their lives to protect the herd from the attack of the Wolves.

I do not think you can break down society any better than that. These are the three basic life-forms we are dealing with, and you need to decide which one you want to be. To learn more about yourself and how you fit into society, I highly recommend you add the book *On Combat* by Lt. Col. Grossman to your officer safety library. It will provide valuable insight and help you understand the world around you.

As a law enforcement officer or a member of our military, I believe you have already made your choice and consider yourself a Sheep Dog. You must be mentally prepared to take on the role of a Sheep Dog because you now have a serious responsibility to protect the weak. You must definitely be willing to confront society's Wolves when necessary. You have told yourself that going to work every day is not a game but truly a matter of life and death. There is no such thing as second place; you must come out a winner if you expect to survive.

The same mental preparation will also help you when you are off-duty. You need to understand the dangers of the world are out there at all times, not just when you are working. A true Sheep Dog is always on duty and prepared to react when necessary.

Sun Tzu recognized that to survive and defeat the enemy you must be mentally involved in the battle. He wrote, ***Now in order to kill the enemy, our men must be roused to anger.*** The soldiers of his time needed a purpose, and they had to be willing to fight to defend it. In your own "battle" you need to understand that "bad" is attacking "good" and you are the one that can make a difference in correcting that. Once you have this desire to get involved, you will be "roused to anger" like Sun Tzu's soldiers. You will see that a "wrong is being committed," and you will be able to defeat that enemy. By not having this attitude you will become complacent, which will open you up for possible failure.

There are countless examples of officers who have been assaulted and survived after receiving horrendous wounds. They survived because they had the mental toughness to work through the problem and realized they had something to live for. They were "roused to anger" because they did not want the bad guy to win. Then, on the other hand, there are accounts of officers receiving relatively minor wounds that succumbed to their injuries and died. You have to wonder if these officers prepared themselves mentally for the dangers of the job.

Read the case study presented in this chapter regarding Sgt. Marcus Young and you will discover someone who truly has a winning mind-set. He was wounded multiple times during a gunfight, including being shot in the head, and in the end he prevailed and the suspect failed. It was an honor for me to meet and listen to Sgt. Young tell his story. He is truly an inspiration when it comes to having a positive winning mind-set.

It is also important to realize in a high-risk situation that everyone will feel some level of fear about what might happen. The appropriate level of fear is actually a good thing and can help you survive the situation you are facing.

There are several types of fear but the most common type results in an increase in your anxiety level because of the potential of injury or death. Once you realize its effects, you can work with it in a positive way.

One positive aspect of fear is that it raises your Situational Awareness regarding almost every aspect of the incident you may find yourself in. This simply means you become hypervigilant and aware of what is happening around you. This is an integral part of dealing with potential danger.

However, if you let irrational fear completely take over, it will paralyze you in your decision making abilities. This will lead to mistakes or inaction, which will limit your ability to succeed. A perfect example of fear taking over is a deer caught in the headlights of a rapidly approaching vehicle. The deer is startled and scared by the lights of the speeding vehicle and freezes in the roadway. The poor deer fails to act and ends up being struck by the vehicle and killed. You do not want to be like that deer caught in the light. You want to react properly and not let your fear prevent you from crossing the road or completing your task.

One way that some people control their fear is by channeling it into anger. This can be tricky because if your fear goes past anger and turns to sheer rage you will make mistakes that could be costly. However, by having a good understanding about the situation you are in and about yourself, your anger may propel you past the barrier that fear has set up for you.

By constantly working on developing your Winning Mind-Set through training and analyzing all of your real world experiences, you will be well on your way to a successful and safe career. Your mind-set is more important than any piece of equipment you could bring with you. Anyone can carry a gun, but you must have the mental toughness to use it. Sun Tzu also understood this when he wrote *Hence the experienced soldier, once in motion, is never bewildered; once he has broken camp, he is never at a loss.*

Key Points

- Develop your winning mind-set.

- Be the sheep dog.

- Recognize fear and work with it.

- Do not let your anger turn to rage.

Case Study
The Marcus Young Incident

I first heard of this incident while I was involved with our Explorer (Cadet) Program. This incident involved a young police explorer who was doing a ride along with Sgt. Marcus Young. When the details of the incident started to emerge, the other advisors I was meeting with began to realize what a dramatic incident had just occurred, especially for the young explorer. The incident shows the dangers involved with police work on any call we may get and it's a great learning tool for officers serious about improving their own safety.

The incident began as a simple petty theft call at a local shopping center that Sgt. Young intended to use to expose his explorer to a theft investigation. Sgt. Young took custody of the female shoplifter without incident and was escorting her to his patrol vehicle along with his Explorer and the store security officer who made the original arrest. Sgt. Young was told that the security officer had seen the female arrestee's boyfriend in the area and that he looked like he had spent time in prison (ascertained by visible tattoos). Young asked the arrestee if her boyfriend was going to cause problems and if he was armed. She answered "no" to both questions. When Sgt. Young got to his patrol vehicle he secured the arrestee in the back seat and then noticed a male subject quickly approaching his location on foot. The subject was a career criminal and a violent white supremacist gang member. As a teenager, he had committed a murder during a robbery and was currently wanted for a home invasion robbery. Sgt. Young moved toward the suspect and ordered him to take his hands out of his pockets. The suspect did not comply and yelled back, "Why?" Sgt. Young again ordered him to remove his hands and asked him what he had in his pockets. The suspect replied that he had a knife and was now two steps from Sgt. Young. He also began making a drawing motion with his arm. Sgt. Young advanced on the suspect, grabbed his arm and attempted to get him into a control hold. The suspect completed his draw and, before Sgt. Young could react, produced a gun instead of a knife and shot Sgt. Young in the face with a snubnose .38 revolver. Sgt. Young was stunned but not out of the fight. He grabbed the suspect and slammed him onto the hood of a parked vehicle. During the struggle Sgt. Young was shot three more times in the upper body. Two of the rounds would have been fatal if not for his body armor. The third round tore through his arm. During the struggle, Sgt. Young and the suspect rolled to the ground. At this point the security officer engaged in the fight and grabbed the suspect and was able to get the gun away from him. The security officer attempted a contact shot to the suspect's head but the suspect's weapon would not fire. It was empty. The security officer threw the gun away and started to punch the suspect. The suspect then produced a large hunting knife and drove it deep into the guard's upper chest striking his lung.

Sgt. Young attempted to draw his handgun but was unable to because of his arm injury. After stabbing the guard, the suspect rushed to Sgt. Young's patrol vehicle, climbed in and closed the door. The suspect did not try to drive away, which startled Sgt. Young. Sgt. Young then realized the suspect was looking for the switch to unlock the HK 33 Assault Rifle that was mounted in the roof rack. Sgt. Young yelled for the explorer to come to him. The Explorer had not fled and was behind cover next to a nearby car. The Explorer came to Sgt. Young and assisted him in drawing his handgun. The Explorer placed the weapon in Sgt. Young's hand. Sgt. Young fired two rounds into the patrol car door in hopes they would penetrate. When the rounds did not reach the suspect, Sgt. Young fired again through the window and was able to strike the suspect in the head. However, it was not a fatal wound. The round glanced off the suspect's forehead and caused him to roll over. Sgt. Young's final round struck the suspect in the buttocks. The round traveled up his spine and stopped near his neck. The fight was now over.

Both Sgt. Young and the security officer recovered from their injuries. Sgt. Young was forced to medically retire, but he went on to earn a Master's Degree and now teaches police science. He also lectures across the country about this incident.

Sgt. Young, the Explorer and the security guard all received numerous awards for their heroism. In addition, Sgt. Young also received the Presidential Medal of Valor from President George W. Bush.

Many of Sun Tzu's principles are in play here, but I think one of the important ones deals with Sgt. Young's mind-set. He was not about to lose to this guy, even after being shot multiple times.

He became enraged and demanded from himself that he would end this fight. Sun Tzu states, *Now in order to kill the enemy, our men must be roused to anger.* Sgt. Young was certainly roused to anger after being assaulted and seeing the security officer stabbed. Sgt. Young continued the fight to stop the threat, which ended in the death of Beckman.

When speaking of a winning mind-set, it is important to remember your goal is to win at all costs. There are no rules and there is no second place when your life is on the line. Sun Tzu understood this also when he wrote, *Therefore, the clever combatant imposes his will on the enemy, but does not allow the enemy's will to be imposed on him.*

Chapter 2   Know Your Levels of Force

> *In battle, there are not more than two methods of attack—the direct and the indirect; yet these two in combination give rise to an endless series of maneuvers.*
>
> —Sun Tzu (Giles)

Other than law enforcement, there are very few professions, if any, that have given its members a greater responsibility than that of using force on its own citizens, including the use of deadly force, in a legal and legitimate manner. What makes this interesting is that this unique ability is granted to us by the same people that the force we employ may actually be used against. However, along with this ability to use force comes a great amount of responsibility that citizens obviously expect us to exercise.

A single incident when force is applied that is eventually deemed unjustified, and even the ones that are justified, can send shock waves throughout your community, your state, the nation and possibly the world. With the advent of social media, the public will look at a particular incident and pass judgment based on their bias before all of the facts are known. Incidents like the Ferguson Shooting and the Freddie Gray Incident in Baltimore illustrate this point perfectly.

As I worked on completing this book I noticed that on an almost weekly, if not daily, basis, a new controversy arises when a police officer's use of force is caught on video. Even before an incident can be fully investigated, special interest groups and the generally uninformed jump to conclusions based on what they want the narrative to be.

(I am still waiting for an apology from then President Obama and his Attorney General Eric Holder regarding their pre-determination of what actually happened in Ferguson, Missouri.)

Even today, I am sure there are very few people who have not heard of the Rodney King Incident that occurred in 1991. During the arrest, two officers repeatedly struck King multiple times with batons until he finally complied with their commands. This incident was caught on video, which eventually led to the officers being prosecuted in court. After the officers were acquitted of any criminal acts, the public outcry over this event led to the 1992 Los Angeles area riots. These riots ended in the deaths of 53 people along with 2000 serious injuries. Besides the human toll, over 1,000 buildings and businesses were vandalized and looted. To quell the riots, just over 10,000 National Guard troops were activated. The total cost associated with the riots was estimated to be in excess of $1 billion. This was also one of the first cases of a police use of force incident being videotaped and then given to the media first, where only select portions of the event were broadcast before the full story could be released. Because of the famous nature of this one incident, it continues to be repeatedly brought up when it comes to the topic of use of force, even though it occurred over 25 years ago.

On January 1, 2009, the unintentional shooting of a resistive subject by Officer Mehserle on the train platform of a Bay Area Rapid Transit Station in Oakland, California, during a New Year's disturbance caused national outrage and questioned law enforcement Use of Force training. This incident, which was caught on cell phone video and immediately broadcast to the world, also highlighted the issue of race. Conclusions were drawn by the uninformed before all of the facts of the incident were known and analyzed. Ultimately, this case did not show any malice. Instead, the evidence demonstrated that it was actually a training issue with Officer Mehserle, who, while under stress, thought he was deploying his newly issued Taser but had inadvertently accessed his handgun. With the ability to record and instantly broadcast an incident caught on video worldwide, the media and other sources are quick to label incidents as inappropriate or illegal without truly understanding what may have actually happened. Be prepared for this consequence and act as if you are always being filmed, because in reality you probably are.

Because of all of the moral and legal obligations involved, officers must be well versed on the reasonable and legal use of force. This includes everything from how to properly employ a specific device such as a Taser or a defensive tactics control hold, to documenting the incident and knowing your legal justifications. It is important to remember that an term *reasonable* applies to that of an officer given the appropriate level of training and experience—not that of a layman fresh off the streets.

Most law enforcement officers have seen some sort of Force Continuum Chart, which describes what a particular level of force is and when it is appropriate to use it. Some feel a chart like this is inherently flawed, because it gives the impression that to progress up the chart, all levels must be attempted. This is not the case and should never be taught as such. Instead, what these charts show are response options that are reasonable for various threats. You are the one who needs to be aware of all the levels of force you have at your disposal and select which one is appropriate for the threat you are facing.

Let's look at what these different levels of force are, starting with the lowest level—your mere presence. Just by walking in to a public location such as a shopping mall or a restaurant, for example, citizens tend to act just a little different when they see you in uniform. Because you do not know when someone is watching you, it is important to project a professional image at all times. Besides the general public, suspects are also sizing you up as soon as they see you. They are asking themselves if you are someone they are willing to confront, or an officer they want to stay clear of. By projecting a professional image in public, you have just exerted a minimal level of force that can alter the actions of others. This is also known as "command presence." Good command presence reflects the confidence you have in yourself and your abilities.

When you move to the next level, verbal commands, you will find that you can usually gain compliance in most situations. Most citizens are law abiding and will recognize your authority and act accordingly. Then there are those who will test this level and push your buttons to try to get a reaction out of you, which they can exploit. Be careful when you start to engage verbally, because if you do not assess your situation appropriately and use too strong of a voice, use profanity or give the wrong commands, you can and will escalate the situation to an unintended level. It is interesting to note that some agencies have recognized that in certain situations, the use of profanity is a specific use of force that is required. To keep their officers from facing complaints, agencies have incorporated clauses in their Use of Force policies that allow certain types of profanity in clearly defined situations. A police officer's greatest and most used weapon should be his or her ability to talk people into compliance. (It is hoped, without the use of profanity.)

Of course, verbal commands do not always work and greater levels of force are often needed. Officers should, therefore, be proficient in their physical defensive tactics skills, which include control-hold techniques for both passive and active resisters. By demonstrating your confidence and willingness to make contact with a subject who is a passive resister, you might gain compliance without having to go hands on and escalate the contact. If that does not work, you must be ready to react to take the person into custody and do it in a way that keeps you, and even the suspect, from getting hurt.

You need to be decisive in your decision making when it comes to going hands-on with a subject. In the military they teach a basic concept of "Speed, Surprise, Violence of Action." Sun Tzu also wrote about this concept when he stated, ***Therefore the good fighter will be terrible in his onset, and prompt in his decision.*** What is basically said here is that once you have made the decision to move in, do so quickly and aggressively so you can gain immediate control. You do not want to give the suspect a chance to set up and prepare a counterassault. Remember to always use the appropriate level of force for the situation you are in.

If you choose a particular control hold and it is not working, it is time to abandon that technique and move on. Remember that *nothing* works 100% of the time. You need to be prepared for such a contingency and have other options available.

Your next level of force should be some sort of compliance tool such as pepper spray or an electronic control device such as a Taser. You need to understand the positives and negatives of whatever tool you have available. I personally have never liked using close-in chemical agents. They always seem to find unintentional targets to irritate and the aftereffects can be troublesome. There are also a fair number of people out there who are not affected by chemical sprays and are able to fight their way through an exposure. This is one of the reasons law enforcement officers are exposed to chemical agents in training. Officers need to know they can fight through it and how the agents affect them. (It is not just for the amusement of the instructors.)

However, I am a firm believer in the use of Tasers or similar tools. They have been proven successful time and time again. Tasers, also known as Electronic Control Devices (ECDs), have allowed officers to take resistive and violent offenders into custody without initially having to go hands-on, which has reduced the number of injuries to both officers and suspects. You must be aware of your target areas when deploying ECDs, because the darts themselves can cause injuries if they strike an unintended target such as the eyes or genitalia. It is also important to know the techniques that can counter the application of a Taser, such as twirling a towel in front of you, which can divert the darts before they make contact. Of course, there are also operator errors that occur that prevent the darts from making contact. This is why receiving proper training in the use of the Taser is very important before you deploy with it.

The next level up if your compliance tools are unavailable or ineffective is impact weapons. Depending on what your agency allows, you may have a straight baton, expandable baton, PR-24, nunchuks or a variety of other devices. There are also distance impact weapons that include dedicated projectile launchers such as the SAGE 37 mm launcher or you can use a dedicated shotgun to launch a variety of impact projectiles. You must be proficient with this level of force because it can easily turn into a deadly force instrument if not applied properly. It is also important to remember that these items do not do you any good if you do not have them with you. Many officers do not wear their batons when seated in their vehicles, which cause batons to be left behind all too often.

The use of personal weapons at this level is more appropriate if you need to strike, kick, elbow or punch a suspect. If possible, the use of personal weapons should be avoided because of the increased risk of injury to yourself. But if this is all you have to work with, you should be proficient and confident in your ability to throw a punch, a palm strike, an elbow or a kick. This is an area where sparring is important during training so you can have a better appreciation of what a strike feels like on both the receiving and giving end. After the Academy, most agencies will avoid this type of training because of the increase risks of injury.

Therefore, you may need to seek out your own training to become more proficient.

Sun Tzu recognized that there are a variety of tactics that can be employed when confronting your adversary. Sun Tzu realized there are many ways to influence a battle and complete your objective without a full-on frontal attack. He talks about the quantity of "Indirect Tactics" that are available when he states, *Indirect tactics, efficiently applied, are inexhaustible as Heaven and Earth, unending as the flow of rivers and streams.* These indirect tactics are your force options, from mere presence to impact weapons. Depending on how you chose to utilize them, they will determine the outcome of your encounter

And finally, the highest level of force available to you is the use of deadly force, or direct "tactics." If you find yourself at this level of force, you are no longer in an arrest situation. It is now a matter of your survival or that of someone else's. You must be prepared for this switch, both mentally and physically, which is where all of your training comes into play.

The most common implement we use to deploy deadly force are firearms and, more specifically, handguns; however, once you have reached this level in a confrontation, it is important to realize that now anything goes. Your objective is to survive at all costs.

Firearms training is very important, but so is a good foundation in unarmed defensive tactics. I feel that some officers have become too reliant on their handgun and think it is the end all to prevent an assault. While training officers in defensive tactics over the years I have asked several what they would do if faced with a subject armed with a knife that is attacking them at a close distance. "I'd shoot 'em" is the standard answer. Good answer if you have established a good reactionary gap and now have time and distance on your side. But when we role-played a scenario in which the suspect being interviewed by the officer suddenly produces an edged weapon and attacks from close range, the officers who do not practice unarmed defensive tactics are usually cut up pretty badly before they can respond with their handguns, if at all.

Officers who actually practice a variety of defensive tactics are usually better prepared for a sudden attack and will respond appropriately. Eventually, most will be able to deploy their handguns after stopping the initial attack. This point was emphasized in the classic training tape by Caliber Press called *Surviving Edged Weapons,* which was released in 1988. This is an excellent training tape and should be required viewing for all police officers. The material is still highly relevant today.

The objective of using deadly force is not to kill your adversary but to stop the threat. However, that is a potential outcome when deadly force is used. When using a firearm, whether a handgun or a rifle, good hits on your target are required. There is no magic one-shot stopper; therefore, be prepared for follow-up shots if necessary, if your adversary still poses a threat. Do not assume just because a subject is shot that he is no longer a deadly threat. Less than 10% of people who suffer gunshot wounds actually end up dying. Of that 10%, very few are instantaneous. There can be several seconds or even minutes before someone succumbs to their injuries, during which time they can still be a serious threat.

Sun Tzu recognized the various levels of force and the myriad of options soldiers (officers) have. He speaks of "normal force or indirect force," which would be our presence and verbal commands; that is, things we use every day in our interactions with the public. He mentions "extraordinary force or direct force," which would be our response to deadly force situations. Then there is everything in between. Sun Tzu gives another example regarding energy that can be used for an analogy for the use of force by using colors when he states, ***There are not more than five primary colors (blue, yellow, red, white and black), yet in combination they produce more hues than can ever be seen.*** Think of all of your force options as the colors and you can see how this analogy applies to modern law enforcement.

Officers must train and prepare themselves to operate in a variety of situations because a simple citizen contact can easily go from good to bad in a matter of seconds, and your life depends on your ability to respond. If you do survive your use of force encounter, your legal survival can depend on your choice of force options and how well they were applied. This all falls back on you, your training and how well you have prepared beforehand.

Sun Tzu recognized the importance of utilizing force in battle and the variety of options available. He writes, ***In all fighting, the direct method may be used for joining battle, but indirect*** *methods will be needed to secure victory.* He then follows that statement with *indirect tactics, efficiently applied, are inexhaustible as Heaven and Earth, unending as the flow of rivers and streams.* All of that is irrelevant if you do not train and prepare ahead of time.

Key Points

- Be aware of the different levels of force.

- Know the ramifications involved in the use of force.

- Become proficient and train at all levels.

- Be prepared to use whatever justifiable level of force is necessary to win.

Chapter 3   Understand Contact and Cover

> *Forming a single united body, it is impossible for either the brave to advance alone, or for the cowardly to retreat alone.*
>
> —Sun Tzu (Giles)

One of the single most important developments in officer safety was the introduction of the principles of Contact and Cover, which occurs when at least two officers handle an encounter. One officer makes "contact" and actually handles the call while the second officer protects the primary officer by providing "cover." Thanks to the work of Steve Albrecht of the San Diego Police Department and John Morison who wrote *Contact and Cover: Two Officer Suspect Control* in 1992, the concept of Contact and Cover changed officer safety tactics for the better and continues to save officers' lives today.

Unfortunately, before the concept was taught on a regular basis at police academies and individual departments, officers were being assaulted and killed on a regular basis by failing to apply this simple principle. Officers were handling calls by themselves and would miss threats that a cover officer would have reacted to.

When an officer arrives at a call for service or makes a traffic stop, there is no way a single officer can keep track of everything at the scene that can pose a threat and cause damage, especially while interacting with people. There are just too many variables to account for. Although most citizen contacts and traffic stops can be handled by a single officer who is mentally aware of and knowledgeable of danger signs, there are always exceptions. By developing your "combat mind-set" you are enhancing the use of all your senses. This includes your sixth sense. This is where the little voice in the back of your head starts talking to you, telling you something bad could happen or is starting to happen. Listen to that little guy and call for a second officer. Do not hesitate to request one and then stand by until the officer arrives. There is usually no need to rush the call. Time is on your side.

After the second officer arrives on scene he or she becomes your cover officer and has but one purpose according to the Contact and Cover principle. Just like it sounds, he or she is your Cover, whose sole responsibility is to watch over you and the scene to ensure your safety. While you are issuing a citation to a traffic violator or taking a subject into custody, your focus should be on the subject you are dealing with. Your cover officer should be checking the surrounding areas for any potential threats. During a traffic stop for instance, if there are additional subjects in the vehicle you have stopped, that should be his or her primary focus. Are other people from the neighborhood coming out to see what you are doing? Is traffic getting too close? The cover officer should be looking for anything that can interfere with your contact or do you harm

The second officer on scene must know and understand his or her role and avoid becoming distracted in an effort to be helpful to the primary officer by contacting passengers, taking statements, filling out forms or doing other errands. Unfortunately, when this happens, a violation of the Contact and Cover principle occurs and a savvy criminal will see his opportunity to divide and conquer. Sun Tzu also recognized this principle when he wrote, *If his forces are united, separate them.* Be aware that the same principle works the same for the bad guy.

The helpful cover officer is now an additional contact officer and his attention is directed away from you and toward whomever or whatever he is dealing with. If the call you are on does in fact require two officers, request a third officer to respond to cover the first two. If the suspect or suspects are able to divide your attention they now have the opportunity to hide something, escape or even assault you.

While studying military tactics, Sun Tzu recognized that when two soldiers are united they can advance together and be victorious. The same concept applies to law enforcement officers. To be victorious in our contacts we must survive them unharmed, and the best way to do that is to have a cover officer watching over you. Sun Tzu also understood that when soldiers (officers) are united, their confidence (hence their courage) increases and they will want to advance. For example, officers conducting a traffic stop with multiple subjects in the vehicle will now feel comfortable about securing consent to search the vehicle. This action alone could lead to arrests that might not have come about if the officer was acting alone. Without the cover officer present, a single officer puts himself in a position of great danger when dealing with multiple subjects that he cannot adequately control.

Sun Tzu also wrote, ***He who exercises no forethought but makes light of his opponents is sure to be captured by him.*** This is sound advice that should be followed. Take the time to plan ahead. Ask for and then wait for your cover officer before making contact. Do not just assume everything is going to be okay. When a solo officer takes action on his own, it's known as "Tombstone Courage." This often occurs when you are familiar with a subject and have dealt with him in the past. Don't assume he will always act the same way. Today's encounter could be very different from those of the past.

Whenever you have the luxury of a cover officer, use it. It is his or her job to assist you in conducting your contact and providing you with an extra set of eyes, and an extra weapon for that matter. The use of a cover officer will greatly reduce or even eliminate the possibility you will end up a victim of an assault during your contact.

Key Points

- Assess your situation and ask for a cover officer if needed.

- Two (or more) officers is always better than just one.

- The Cover Officer should provide cover only and not get involved with the call.

- Do not underestimate your adversary.

Chapter 4   Survive Searches and Suspect Contacts

> *Therefore the clever combatant imposes his will on the enemy, but does not allow the enemy's will to be imposed on him.*
>
> —Sun Tzu (Giles)

Whenever you find yourself searching for a suspect, for example, whether it is in a room or in an open area, you need to realize that you are moving into his territory. He is likely familiar with the layout of the rooms, any hiding places, escape routes and potential ambush sites. Even if it is his first time there, he has still been there longer than you.

If you find yourself in a foot chase, suspects will run from you in the hope that you will pursue them into areas where they have the advantage, which will allow them to either escape, hide or ambush you. They may also attempt to separate you from your partner, and therefore your cover officer. In fact, many Departments now require specific training on conducting foot pursuits to improve officers' tactics. According to a study by the Los Angeles County Sheriff's Office, close to 25% of their deadly force encounters involved some sort of a foot pursuit during the event.

Sun Tzu noted that the one more skilled in the tactic of dividing his enemy will win on the field of battle when he wrote, **If his forces are united, separate them.** Therefore you must understand and recognize when it is being employed against you. Once you recognize the tactic you can and should employ it to succeed.

Let us use a building search as an example of how Sun Tzu's principles apply to modern day law enforcement. You are checking the exterior of a building after responding to an alarm call and you find an open door that appears to be an oversight. After being told there is no K-9 available, you and your partner enter the building and as he provides cover as you move forward down the hall. Suddenly, a suspect appears at the end of the hall, sees you and bolts into a nearby room. At this point, you ask for

27

additional units to set up a perimeter around the building to prevent an escape if you have not done so already. Depending on the number of rooms between you and the suspect, you will need to get additional resources to clear and hold those rooms while you advance to the last known location of the suspect. When you reach that room, you issue a verbal command for the suspect to show himself. Now is the time to recognize and understand where the field of battle is, where it begins and who controls what. Now is also the time to slow down and take a deep breath. If there is no response, you start to "cut the pie" to get a better look into the room. You spot the suspect behind a desk and order him to stand up. He complies with your commands. *Do not* focus solely on the one suspect and rush into the room in a hurry to handcuff him because you are entering his space. There is always the possibility of a second suspect preparing to ambush you from an unknown location.

We see this need to rush in and take the suspect into custody primarily with new and inexperienced officers, but it can happen to any of us when we are caught up in the moment and all of our adrenaline is flowing. It is important to take a moment and assess the situation. This is not the time to get so focused you lose track of everything else. When you make contact with the suspect, control the situation and order the suspect to face away from you and move backward toward your location. Get him to come to you and the area that you control. Have the suspect exit the room and secure him from behind a position of cover. Your cover officer should be in a position to watch over you and the room. Once he is secured, do not forget the valuable resource of asking him where his partner is. (Remember to ask as if you know there is someone else.) Who knows, he might tell you. Hand the suspect over to additional support officers before continuing on. Again, you do not want to be divided in your responsibilities of handling a suspect and searching the building. Eventually you, or someone else, will still need to enter and clear the room.

Prior to entering a room start cutting the pie at the doorway to try and get a visual on as much of the room as you can. If available, small handheld mirrors are always handy to check around corners or in through doorways. If you have the luxury of a robot or a pole camera, use it. Be sure to practice using your mirror or any other piece of equipment before the time comes when you actually have to. Knowing how to hold the mirror and your handgun correctly takes a bit of practice to do it right.

Enter the room after you have cleared it the best you can from outside. Check your hard corners first, which are the corners to your immediate right and left and are the most difficult locations to clear from outside while slicing the pie. Of course, if you have an immediate threat upon entering, deal with that first, but you will still have to check the hard corners for any additional suspects. If there is no immediate threat, you will then need to do a systematic search of the room. Your cover officer should be doing just that, covering you while you search. The cover officer should remain stationary and assume a solid position of advantage while you are searching. A stationary shooter is always more accurate than one that is moving and can provide a better response to a threat. Before you begin, decide if you will search the entire room or if you will switch roles and split the room. You will then cover your partner while he searches the other half. If you do switch roles make sure that you communicate to ensure that no area is missed. Once the room is clear your job is still not done. You will need to continue on with your partner and search the remainder of the building to include attic and basement crawl spaces, storage areas, closets and restrooms. Once you complete your primary search, do a secondary detailed search. There will always be places you miss on the first go through that a suspect can hide in. If you have to return to a location that was searched then abandoned for some reason, reenter and search again as if it was the first time. Do not assume that area is still clear.

One more thought about searches for suspects. You should always search as if you expect to find someone. Be mentally prepared in every corner, under every bed, in every closet and bathroom and in every room to find the suspect. Be relieved when you do not find someone and move on. Do not be surprised when you do find him hiding. If you are startled, he will then have the advantage of surprise and will momentarily control the situation and that might be all the time he needs.

Another common example in which you will find officers rushing into a situation involving suspect contacts is after a vehicle pursuit. During the pursuit your adrenaline will be pumping with everything that is going on and tunnel vision is hard to avoid. As the suspect vehicle crashes or comes to a stop, avoid rushing to the vehicle to get your hands on the suspect. Too many of us want to run up to the car and pull the driver out of the window and deposit him on the ground. Take a deep breath and assess what you have. Again, avoid being sucked in. The offender is obviously considered dangerous so take some necessary precautions. Be cautious about deciding who to chase if multiple suspects flee the vehicle in different directions and you are alone. If you choose to chase the driver, his partners may circle behind you. If the suspect, or suspects, remains in the vehicle, you need to utilize good officer safety tactics and stay behind cover until backup arrives. Establish fields of fire on the vehicle and then order the suspects out of the vehicle one at a time. Bring the suspects back to you and the area you control. There is no need to go forward into the danger zone between your vehicle and his. If he fails to comply and stays in the vehicle, the situation is still under control. You have time on your side and can treat the situation as a barricaded suspect.

If the suspect flees from the vehicle on foot, he may be trying to get you to run past his vehicle, which may still contain a hidden partner. Take the time to check the vehicle and then pursue. Be cautious and consider setting up a perimeter instead of chasing blindly. The majority of fleeing suspects will take to the ground and hide once they lose track of a pursuing officer. Once you have a perimeter set up, then you can search in a systematic manner and slowly take control of areas. Utilize all of your resources such as air support and K-9 units if available. When you contact the suspect, always bring him to you and the area you control.

A basic military concept we should all follow is that if you control the ground (or field of battle) you have the advantage. It applied 2,500 years ago and it still applies today in both the military and law enforcement. Remember this basic principle and it will greatly increase your survival chances when searching for and contacting suspects.

Sun Tzu issues a warning about evaluating your enemy, but it also applies in reverse when the suspect is evaluating you. He writes, ***If he is secure at all points, be prepared for him. If he is in superior strength, evade him.***

Key Points

- Do NOT chase a suspect into unknown territory.

- Stay with your partner and provide cover for each other.

- Bring the suspect to you and the area you control.

- Always assume there is another suspect.

- Be mentally prepared and expect to find the suspect when you search.

Chapter 5   Off-Duty Survival

> *One defends when his strength is inadequate;*
> *he attacks when it is abundant.*
> —Sun Tzu

From our first days at the academy and throughout our careers we constantly train and prepare for our on-duty encounters, which is because this is where we are actually being dispatched to calls involving violence and the potential for violence. In fact, in 2017 over 60,200 law enforcement officers were feloniously assaulted according to FBI statistics and 46 were murdered while on-duty. By being dispatched to known calls, we can prepare ourselves while en route to react to any threat. We train to use our available equipment and we know that if we need help it is usually en route, because a cover officer was already dispatched. If we find that we still need additional help it is a radio call away and the cavalry is on the way.

But what happens at the end of your shift when you leave your duty belt, ballistic vest and radio in the locker and head home? Are you still prepared to deal with threats? There are some officers who believe that once the uniform is off, so are they. These officers seem to have a mental switch they turn off that prevents them from facing the ever-present threats of the real world.

If you read the annual LEOKA reports published by the FBI, you will find numerous examples of officers attacked and killed while off-duty. We all have to remember that bad things happen out there to anyone and the potential that you will be involved in an off-duty encounter is greater than ever.

There are many examples of off-duty officers being followed home, assaulted and killed. Officers have been recognized while off-duty by criminals they have had previous contact with and attacked by them. In May 2013 an off-duty officer in Kentucky was ambushed on his way home. He had stopped to remove some debris from a roadway that was apparently left there deliberately and was shot in the head with a shotgun by an unknown suspect.

You must prepare for these encounters just as you do for your on-duty encounters. In fact, I would argue you should prepare more because you have less at your disposal and more on the line if something goes wrong.

Your "always prepared" off-duty mind-set should always be switched on when you are not at work. Most police officers I know still think like cops when off duty. They look at people and make immediate assessments of them. What are they wearing? How are they acting? Who are they with? They notice things that are out of the ordinary and they trust their sixth sense. Some may call this stereotyping, but it is really taking into account all of your acquired knowledge and making an educated assessment. Everyone already does this in some way. Remember the last time you boarded a plane with unassigned seating. How did you choose your seat? What criteria did you use to decide who you wanted to sit next to for the next couple of hours? You made a split second decision based primarily on what you saw. An excellent book I highly recommend for you to read that covers these split-second decisions and how they are made is called *Blink* written by Malcolm Gladwell.

Officers with good off-duty safety sense also have a tendency to watch their backs and sit in public places where they can see who is approaching them. This is called having good "situational awareness." It is important to always be aware of your surroundings so you can react appropriately to any potential threats. However, just watching your back is certainly not enough, but it is a great starting point in preparing your off-duty mind-set.

As police officers, we have a moral and legal obligation to act when on-duty when we see a wrong being dealt to someone, but how we react can be completely different when we are off-duty and have our children next to us than when we are on-duty and have a fully armed and trained police officer at our side.

I believe Sun Tzu recognized and understood this when he said that you should **defend when your strength is inadequate**. When you are with your family and you on-view a robbery or other violent crime, and you are not directly threatened by the suspect, you should really consider whether or not to engage the suspect or just be a great witness. I remember hearing a story of an off-duty officer walking through a strip mall with his young daughter. He saw a suspect fleeing a bank and told his daughter to hunker down behind a parked car while he went to stop the guy. When the suspect's partner, who was in the getaway car, saw this, he shot the daughter to distract the officer. Ask yourself, was intervention worth it for that officer?

It obviously all changes when you and your family become the focus of the suspect's attention. Are you prepared to defend them and have you prepared them to assist in their own defense? This all involves preplanning on your part to prepare your family on what to expect. This is not the time when you want your significant other or your children to argue with you when you yell for them to get down. This is the time when immediate action on everyone's part could mean the difference between getting someone hurt and getting out of the situation unscathed. In regard to off-duty encounters, another Sun Tzu maxim that applies here states, ***Move not unless you see an advantage; fight not unless the position is critical.*** I would suggest that if your family is threatened the situation is extremely "critical."

You can never know when you might find yourself in a situation off-duty that you did not plan on. Because of this, you need to better your odds of avoiding off-duty conflict by not inadvertently bringing the situation upon yourself. This could easily happen if you are recognized as an off-duty cop by the way you dress or how you talk. With the popularity of civilian "tactical pants," police t-shirts and hats, it is not hard to pick out some people in a crowd as police officers. Look at how off-duty fireman dress with their high profile FIRE DEPT blue shirts. Law enforcement officers should also be able to show our pride for our profession in public, but if we do so in the wrong environment, we can easily become a target. I have to admit that I like the pants and shirts, but I also use caution and common sense on how I dress for where I am going.

Another giveaway that you are a law enforcement officer is the way you carry your weapon off-duty. (You do have one, right?!) You may think you have your weapon concealed but the way it "prints" in your clothing when you move may give its location away. "Printing" is when you can see the outline of the weapon through your shirt or jacket. If your clothing is too tight and you move a certain way, your weapon will stand out. Also, wearing the famous fanny pack from the 1980s and '90s is almost a sure give away. I know it is a comfortable way to carry your weapon, but it screams "cop." Fortunately, this trend is going away.

Remember, if the bad guy thinks you are a law enforcement officer you will become his biggest threat and the first thing he wants to eliminate. Try to keep a low profile and do not stand out.

Speaking of carrying a weapon off duty, you need to carry one if you are serious about your safety and that of your family. I have heard officers tell me that they only carry off-duty when they "go to bad places." Really! How can you possibly tell nothing bad will happened where you are going? How many assaults have occurred in shopping malls, restaurants, sporting events, amusement parks, and even churches for that matter? All of these places could be considered "safe."

When you think about the three basic viewpoints that Lt. Col. Grossman accurately describes in his books and presentations— the Sheep, the Wolves and the Sheep Dogs—you need to realize this applies all the time. According to Lt. Col. Grossman, if you can legally carry an off-duty weapon and you choose not to, then when you step outside your house unarmed you might as well stop and say, "BAA   BAA   BAA," because you are no longer a Sheep Dog. You are now just another Sheep among the Wolves.

When you choose an off-duty weapon, you need to make sure it is of a substantial caliber to have an effect on your intended target. I would not recommend anything less than a .380 caliber. I know, a .22 can still hurt the bad guy, but you want a round that can penetrate some clothing or possibly an intermediate barrier and still be somewhat effective. I personally carry either a .9 mm or a .40 cal. with at least 15 rounds of quality duty ammunition. This may mean carrying a spare magazine when I carry a smaller sub compact weapon. Your choice of weapon will also be dependent on the environment you will be in. It is much easier to carry and conceal a full-size handgun during the winter than it would be during the summer. Be sure to practice drawing the weapon from your preferred carry position. You should be able to get your handgun into operation quickly and smoothly, especially from a position of disadvantage.

If you do choose to take action, or are simply forced too, do you have a way of identifying yourself when the good guys arrive? You certainly do not want to get shot by responding officers when they cannot identify you. This happens more often than you might think. At least have your badge with you so that you can display it when the officers arrive on scene and be sure to follow their commands. If you call 9-1-1 before, during or after your confrontation, be sure to give them your description so the dispatchers can relay that information to the responding officers.

Several assaults on police officers have occurred when suspects hell-bent on revenge have followed an officer home and attacked him or her when they feel the officer will be unprepared to react. An example of this was when an officer was ambushed and killed has he entered the garage to his residence after arriving home from work. In early 2018, an off-duty Florida officer arrived home with his family and was robbed in front of his house. The suspect was able to gain control of the officer's weapon and shoot him with his own gun. It is also very important to note that officers' homes have been targets for burglaries because of the arsenals of weapons some officers seem to accumulate.

You should consider what you can do to improve your safety at home. There are a variety of simple things that can be done to harden your home: from installing solid core doors with dead bolts throughout to placing single-push panic buttons in various rooms attached to your alarm system. Designate a safe room, or two, and have more than one means of communication to call for help. Have a good first-aid kit you can get to just in case. Think about your escape routes from your house if using your safe room is not practical. Oh yes, and do not forget the benefit of our big, mean-looking, four-legged friends.

Consider training your family on the use of firearms, especially your significant other. It is important for them to be able to protect themselves if you are not home and also to come to your aid if needed. If the suspects are now encountering more than one armed person they may think twice before continuing.

Do not forget to train your children in the use of firearms when they are old enough to understand why they are being trained and are aware of the consequences of using a firearm. There are several examples of armed 12- and 13-year-olds who were home alone stopping burglars who tried to enter their homes. Your children should at least have some weapon-safety training in case they come across a weapon in the house.

Above all, have a plan for your family. We always hear folks talk about this for natural disasters, fires and so on where they will meet and how they will communicate. Why then don't we plan with our families what we would do if our castle is attacked? Do we have a safe room? Where are the weapons we can get to? Do you have body armor available? What are your escape routes? How do you call for help? These are things to think about before you have to. Now if you cannot get your family to participate in your "paranoid" immediate action drills, you should at least have the plan figured out yourself. Yes, people may call you paranoid, but I would suggest you use the word "prepared."

It is important to prepare yourself for off-duty encounters because the likelihood of being attacked is always present. Recent studies have shown the odds are greater than ever. We certainly do not want to become the Sheep of our society. We need to always be the Sheep Dogs.

When dealing with our officer safety mind-set, especially off-duty, it is important to always remember one of Sun Tzu's principles, ***To secure ourselves against defeat lies in our own hands.*** We are the ones to decide if we are prepared or not to survive.

Key Points

- Train for off-duty encounters.

- Carry a weapon off-duty.

- Keep a low profile.

- Prepare your family with a plan.

Case Study
Trolley Square Shopping Mall Shooting

The night of February 12, 2007, started out normal enough for Ken Hammond. He was at a local shopping mall in Ogden, Utah, with his wife, who was pregnant at the time. They were planning on enjoying a Valentine's dinner at a restaurant in the mall. After dinner they were heading for an overnight stay at a local bed and breakfast.

Little did they know that an 18-year-old suspect named Talovic had just entered the mall with a shotgun with the intent of killing. After dinner, when Ken and his wife were leaving the restaurant, they heard "popping" sounds from the lower level. They assumed it was construction noise and continued on their quest to buy a Valentine's day present. When they heard the noise again, Ken made a comment to his wife that the noise was loud and was bothering him. He looked over the rail to the lower level to see if he could find the source of the noise.

What he saw was not what he expected. Numerous people were lying on the ground, many with obvious injuries. Ken then saw Talovic carrying the shotgun.

Fortunately for the citizens in the mall at that time, Ken was an off-duty six-year veteran of the Utah Police Department. Even on a date with his wife, Ken was armed with a Kimber .45 caliber pistol. Ken immediately went into combat mode and drew his weapon and started yelling for people to get down. The shooter heard Ken yelling and looked up and spotted him. The shooter fired at him. Ken's first thought was pure anger. He recalled, "Who in the hell are you to shoot at me and my wife. I wanted to go down there and kill him with my hands." Ken yelled at his wife to go and secure the restaurant and call 911. Ken's wife, Sarita, was a police dispatcher and knew exactly what information would be needed by the police. She borrowed a cell phone and called 9-1-1. She provided a description of both the suspect and her husband, specifically telling the on-duty dispatcher that her husband was an off-duty police officer and not a second gunman. She added he was actively engaging the suspect.

Ken now had the suspect's full attention. From the lower level the suspect fired at Ken who had moved and then proned out. Ken was not familiar with the mall layout but knew there were escalators behind him. Ken was focused on keeping an eye on the suspect but lost track of him. Ken began to stand up when he saw a civilian pointing to were the suspect had gone. At that time Ken saw the first responding officer, Sgt. Andrew Oblad, and they made eye-contact. Ken said that he was worried Sgt. Oblad would think he was the gunman but after what seemed like several minutes, but was actually only seconds, Sgt. Oblad indicated he knew Ken was a "good guy."

Ken motioned he was coming down the escalator and then joined up with Oblad. Suddenly the suspect fired at the both of them. Ken took cover behind a concrete pillar and then returned fire. Ken was now concerned with the amount of ammunition he had. While Ken was considering his option he suddenly heard additional gunfire that was not the suspect. Additional responding officers had engaged the suspect with semi and automatic gunfire. Ken looked in the direction of the suspect and saw that he was down. He continued to watch has the suspect was taken into custody and then realized the incident was "pretty much over."

Ken estimated the entire episode lasted about three to five minutes. During that time five people were murdered and four others were critically injured.

For Ken's quick action in diverting the suspect's attention, he was rightfully hailed as a hero. Ken had not been involved in a shooting prior to this, and he stated that he was surprised at how "on" he was. He stated all of his on-duty training kicked in and he applied it in an off-duty situation.

Ken's experience is a true reminder that at anytime and at anyplace you can be called upon to act and you should be prepared to execute both mentally and physically. It also reminds us of the need to carry off-duty so you do not become a victim yourself.

Chapter 6   Backup Weapons and Equipment Essentials

> *The good fighters of old first put themselves beyond the possibility of defeat.*
> —Sun Tzu (Giles)

One must always prepare for the worst-case scenario. Failing to do so just sets you up for failure. By recognizing what Sun Tzu thought of as "unfavorable factors," you can prepare in advance.

One area that many officers feel is an important area to prepare and train for is the confrontation with a deadly force situation. This scenario would seem obvious to most, but few officers really take the time to adequately prepare mentally and physically for such an encounter.

During your survival preparation, an important but often overlooked item to consider is that of backups. Most think of "backup" as another officer who provides you cover during a call, which can be true when you are on-duty. However, what about when you find yourself alone on-duty and the only backup you have is yourself and what you brought with you? The term backup now takes on a whole new meaning.

I am a firm believer that if it can go wrong, it will go wrong. If it can break, it will break. If you can lose it, it will get lost. And this will always happen at the worst conceivable time. This phenomenon is commonly referred to as Murphy's Law and it is ever-present and a circumstance that should always be accounted for.

One way to overcome these shortcomings and battle Mr. Murphy is to prepare beforehand. Take inventory of your equipment and see what can break, malfunction or get lost and plan on how you would deal with such an occurrence. A top law enforcement training professional, Gordon Graham, who deals in liability issues coined the phrase, "If it is predictable, it is preventable." To better prepare yourself, take the time to make a prediction about how your equipment might fail and try to figure out a way to prevent your prediction from coming to fruition. The following is a compendium of items that I feel is important for you to consider carrying.

The majority of us work in the dark (physically, not mentally) and will find ourselves operating in low-light situations. Even officers who work only day shift may find themselves in a dark room or warehouse in need of light. Therefore having a good source of light is quite important. Your light should ideally produce at least 250 lumens of light to be useful, although 500-lumen lights or more are actually becoming the norm. Because you will probably be issued a flashlight, bring it with you. But what happens when the battery dies, the switch breaks or the bulb goes out? You better have a backup. With the advent of small, high output lights, there is no excuse not to carry a backup light on your duty belt at all times. They take up little space and you can forget that it is there until you need it. Another good source of light would be your weapon-mounted light. This should be a "mission essential" piece of equipment regardless, because you positively need to identify what you are shooting at in a low-light situation. However, a weapon-mounted light would not be a good light to use during Field Sobriety Tests. You would probably find yourself on YouTube fairly quickly for doing that.

Yes, I said it, three sources of light if you work nights and at least two for day shifters.

Have you ever thought about what you would do if your radio went down? Most of us do not carry a backup police radio. We have access to one in our vehicles, but the chances of being next to your patrol vehicle or being able to get back to it is not very likely during a violent encounter. However, we all carry a cell phone nowadays. If you don't, you should. Make sure you have one with you on calls, and that it is not left in the car. This is important so you can call for help if needed. A good feature of some phones is that they have a GPS locater feature, which could prove useful if you find yourself wounded in an unknown location.

One more word about cell phones. Although they are good to have, they do have one serious drawback: they make noise. Turn the ringer OFF. There is nothing more annoying or dangerous than conducting a stealthy building search and suddenly you hear the ring tone for the phone or the theme song to a Justin Bieber song blaring from your partner's cell phone (or worse, from your phone). The offending party then has to scramble to shut it off as quickly as possible. Talk about a distraction that can divert your attention and possibly give away your position to the bad guy. So, for obvious reasons, just keep your cell phone on Silent.

I would like to say that in almost 30 years I have never seen a pair of handcuffs fail, but I have on multiple occasions. Most of these incidents were purely operator malfunctions, but some were mechanical. There are accounts of suspects under the influence twisting handcuffs so much they were able to separate the strands, thereby freeing themselves. This usually resulted in severely damaging their wrists in the process.

Other failures have occurred when using an inferior brand of handcuffs. The locking mechanism just breaks or the chain snaps.

It is important to remember that handcuffs are not fail proof and can be defeated if the suspect knows how and is given the chance. You should take the time to learn these techniques so you can take precautions to prevent cuff failures from happening. One of the techniques simply requires striking the handcuff against a hard surface, which will bounce the pawl out of the ratchet. If you can do that and pull on the loose arm, the cuff will open, which takes practice but can be done.

Handcuffs also require maintenance because they can rust, which renders them unusable when you might need them. If they do not open smoothly they are just going to be that much harder to get on the suspect, especially if he is not cooperating.

Another major concern with handcuffs is simply running out of them. There will be many times you will find yourself in the need to handcuff multiple suspects or a single, very large suspect. It is always a good practice to carry at least two pair of handcuffs. Weaving a large flex cuff through your duty belt is also a useful solution to not having enough handcuffs. Handcuffs should also be carried where you can get to them with either hand and also when wearing heavy clothing or rain gear. (Don't forget seasonal changes.) I recommend carrying a double handcuff case in front where you have easy access to your handcuffs with both hands. This positioning will also relieve some pressure on your back to help you see retirement. And, finally, don't forget about the keys for your handcuffs. Standard keys are small and easy to lose. I carry a larger key that makes manipulating the key in tight spaces easier. I also carry a backup handcuff key on my key ring. Some officers I know carry an extra hidden handcuff key in case they find themselves restrained by their own handcuffs. This may seem extreme until you find yourself handcuffed. (Remember what Gordon Graham said, "If is predictable. It is preventable.")

Another item that could fail that you probably want functioning 100% of the time is whatever weapon system you are carrying. Even if we maintain and take perfect care of our handgun, rifle or shotgun, things can go wrong. Something could break internally, you could run out of ammo, it could be taken away from you or you could simply lose control of it. (I won't mention the possibility of leaving your weapon in your locker by mistake before hitting the streets—because that never happens.) If any of these situations present themselves, it would be nice to have ready access to a secondary weapon to fight your way out of harm's way.

The backup handgun you carry should be of a sufficient caliber to cause considerable damage. I would not recommend anything smaller than a .380. However, any round can be effective, including 22LR, if they are delivered to the right target areas. The problem with small calibers is that they may not get to the right target areas because of thick clothing or other intermediate barriers.

Many weapon manufacturers such as Glock produce smaller versions of their full-size duty weapon that on some occasions accept the same magazines. Having the same weapon design also helps with manipulation skills and your familiarity with the operating system while under extreme stress. For example, a bad idea would be to carry a full-size Glock for duty use, which has no external safeties, and then carry a 1911-style pistol that requires a safety to be disengaged.

Backup weapons should also be carried where you can get to them in a hurry and with either hand. There are several legitimate locations to choose from, including an ankle holster, inside a concealed pouch on your belt (my partner used a modified handcuff case for a small .25 semi-auto) or attached to your ballistic vest. All have advantages and disadvantages. You need to decide what works for you and then practice.

Make sure you have a secure holster for your backup weapon, which is vitally important if you choose to carry one on your ankle. You do not want it coming loose during a struggle or if you are running.

You also need to get to the weapon with either hand if you find yourself in various positions of disadvantage, such has lying on your back or crouching behind cover. What if you are wrestling with a suspect on the ground? Would you be able to access your weapon that is secured to your vest inside of your shirt?

Most officers I know, including myself, do not carry spare ammunition for our backup weapons. If I have resorted to my backup handgun something has gone very wrong, and I am fighting my way out of a danger zone and retreating to safety. I hope I can do that with 8 rounds at a minimum. If not, extra ammo if you have room would be a good idea. An option to solve the problem of extra ammunition is choosing a weapon system such as a Glock that allows magazines from different sized guns of the same caliber to be used in each weapon. In an extreme situation, you might be forced to download duty magazines and transfer the ammo to your backup weapon if the caliber is the same.

Another popular item officers are carrying more often are knives. The most common style is some type of folding knife clipped to a pants pocket. I have seen many officers carrying knives over the years and have asked them why they carry it and if they have ever trained with it. The most common answers to those questions are, "To cut seat belts" and "No," respectively. The second most common answer is, "To protect myself," but they still do not train with it.

If you are going to carry a knife you need to realize that it is a level of force that can and should be employed if you find it necessary. It is not a primary weapon used when making arrests, but it is a valuable instrument to have access to if you cannot get to your primary or secondary handgun and your life is on the line.

Several years ago I took a class conducted by the Cutting Edge Institute and taught by George Williams. This physically demanding class focused on several points. First, Practice, Practice, Practice. Second, the carry placement of your knife was emphasized. It was suggested that the knife be carried on your non-gun side so you could access it with a support hand while your primary hand secures your weapon in the holster, which prevents a disarm. A viable position is in the waistband concealed behind your duty belt in what is called the "appendix carry position." This location allows for access with both hands. You will find it difficult to draw your knife from your pants pocket with your opposite hand while actually engaged with a suspect.

You should also carefully consider the type of knife you wish to use. If you choose a folding knife, can you open the blade with either hand? Will the blade lock open and stay open? Is the blade sharp enough to get through layers of clothing, and is it sturdy enough not to break? You can still carry an additional folding utility knife for general cutting and prying, which in a sense is a backup knife for your primary survival knife. Another option is a fixed-blade knife. They are a little harder to conceal in a location where you can readily access them if needed. The most common option for concealed carry would be a fixed-blade boot knife, but some officers opt for carrying them attached to their vests.

Remember you are carrying at least two flashlights and two handguns, and you might want to consider carrying two edged weapons. My primary back-up knife is tucked in my waist band and never used for ordinary chores. This is the one my life may depend on. The one clipped in my pants pocket is the one I use when a knife is needed and not an edged weapon. Big difference.

If you decide to carry an edged weapon, be aware of the public perception surrounding using a knife in a deadly force situation. Can you imagine the liberal media headlines, "Officer stabs suspect to death." I hate to have to say it, but there are more politically correct ways to engage threats than others. When it comes down to it, you do what it takes to survive, but it is something you should be aware of. I thought this humorous at first when it was mentioned in class but the more I thought about it, the truer it is. It is best to use your knife to fight your way to your handgun to finish the fight. Better to have the coroner's report say "Cause of Death—Multiple Gun Shot Wounds" than "Cause of Death—Multiple Stab Wounds."

These are just a few examples of things you need for backup. Take the time to plan ahead and see what can go wrong with your equipment and what you can do to minimize that impact. There are countless other example I could have written about, including batteries for your cameras and extra pens, but you know your situation best.

Sun Tzu saw the need to plan ahead and prepare for the enemy when he wrote, *He who exercises no forethought but makes light of his opponents is sure to be captured by him.* The enemy Sun Tzu is talking about here is Mr. Murphy. You want to do everything you can to prevent him from showing up. This is valuable advice to follow when planning anything.

Key Points

- Be aware of Murphy's Law—What can go wrong will go wrong.

- Evaluate all your equipment.

- Prepare to backup everything.

- Practice, Practice, Practice.

Chapter 7   Terrorism Response

> *A kingdom that has once been destroyed can never come again into being; nor can the dead ever be brought back to life.*
>
> —Sun Tzu

Prior to September 11, 2001, everyone had heard about terrorism but the average citizen did not take it seriously. It was something that occurred in far-off lands to "the other guy." Despite famous incidents that caught everybody's attention like the Munich massacre of the Israeli hostages at the 1972 Olympic Games or the 1988 Pan Am Flight 103 bombing over Lockerbie, Scotland, we in America did not think such incidents would occur here on US soil. Even when Americans were the direct victims of terrorist acts, like the 1985 Achille Lauro hijacking in which American Leon Klinghoffer was killed and thrown overboard or the bombing of the Marine barracks in Beirut, Lebanon in which 241 Marines were killed, American law enforcement did not connect the dots and start planning for attacks here at home. We had plenty of warnings and even a few attacks that should have woken us all up. In 1993 the World Trade Center was attacked by al–Qaeda, and we responded with a limited effort to destroy their training camps. Even after this event we still did not start large-scale or local-level preparations.

Unfortunately, like most change, it takes a catastrophic event to propel substantial change in the way law enforcement conducts business. The event I am speaking of became known as "9-11" and cost the lives of nearly 3000 Americans, including 72 police officers. After that attack our nation went on a war footing. Local law enforcement also began to respond when intelligence sources indicated that additional attacks were planned. Previous to 9-11, in response to tragedies such as the first World Trade Center attack in 1993 and the 1995 bombing of the Oklahoma Federal Building, some local, state and federal law enforcement agencies had started to plan for domestic terroristic attacks and many equipped officers with patrol rifles and other response gear, which sped up our capabilities to respond to future terrorist attacks.

Administrators realized that the average patrol officer would be potentially outgunned in the event they encountered a determined terrorist or criminal in the act. Forward-thinking jurisdictions authorized the deployment of patrol rifles and began training their entire departments in their use. They understood the rifle was a much more versatile weapon system than the standard handgun or shotgun.

The need to arm police officers with rifles came to the forefront because of a major event that occurred at a bank in southern California in 1997 in the city of North Hollywood, which showed us how unprepared we were to deal with attacks from heavily armed gunmen, whether domestic criminals or terrorists. In the North Hollywood Shootout, bank robbers armed themselves with multiple, fully automatic weapons and thousands of rounds of ammunition. They had customized ballistic protection that covered their entire bodies. They engaged with responding law enforcement officers who were armed only with handguns and shotguns. An estimated 1100 rounds were fired that day by the suspects and over 650 rounds fired by law enforcement. Officers were forced to obtain high-powered rifles from a local gun store to match the weaponry of the suspects. The suspects were eventually stopped when one was eliminated by responding SWAT personnel with rifles and the other took his own life after one of his weapons was disabled. Amazingly, there were no other fatalities that day (except for the bad guys), but 12 officers were wounded along with 8 civilians.

Because officers were now being equipped with rifles, the mind-set of law enforcement administrators were more open to change. We were identifying potential threats and targets in our jurisdiction and taking that information seriously. We started to plan on how we would respond to a variety of attacks. This also occurred the same time Active Shooter training started to take hold. It got us all in the right mind-set, which is that "standard law enforcement techniques no longer applied." We needed to have a combat mind-set when dealing with these threats.

In my home county in northern California the need for a specialized team was recognized by law enforcement leaders and a regional response team was formed to deal specifically with terroristic style threats. The members of this team were selected from the various SWAT teams in the county who wanted to volunteer and learn a specialized skill in dealing with terrorism and the threat of weapons of mass destruction. I was one of the original members of the team and, at first, the threats out there that we had to train for seemed overwhelming. Over time, we realized that other than wearing our protective suits and lugging around our SCBA Air Tanks, the mission was essentially the same as a standard SWAT operation with only a few exceptions. We had to modify our thinking when it came to our Use of Force Policy and how we applied it. We also had to change the speed in which we operated.

In regard to the speed of our operations, we came to understand that when dealing with a subject that has the ability to release or detonate a WMD, we were really dealing with a Hostage Rescue style operation. The citizens in the community are the hostages and are being held by the risk of a release or a detonation, and we needed to end the threat as fast as possible.

This plays into our Use of Force Policy. At first we thought we would have to re-write the policy but upon reflection there was no need. We were authorized to use deadly force to protect our citizens from death or great bodily injury. How much more of a threat is a WMD to life as that of a lone crazed gunman? It is all a matter of perspective. What we had to discuss was, when does the suicide bomber or devout terrorist become a deadly threat requiring the immediate use of deadly force? There still is no way to put into writing exactly when deadly force can and should be applied because there are too many possible scenarios and writing it all down would make the policy too restrictive and complicated. This would expose all of us to more liability. Having an overly restrictive Rules of Engagement Policy simply does not make sense in this situation. It falls back to common sense, what is reasonable, your training and experience and how you can articulate the need to use force to stop a threat. In my view, once a suicide bomber straps on the vest he is a threat. But what about his handler with a remote activation device? What about the scouts that may be his lookout? If you can justify your actions and can walk away feeling good about what you did morally, I believe Sun Tzu would say you are good to go.

Sun Tzu recognized that soldiers that understood their Moral Law and abided by their beliefs had a better chance of achieving victory. This was the first characteristic Sun Tzu mentions when he lists the 7 conditions to predict victory against your enemy. (Read more about the 7 Conditions in the chapter dealing with Special Response Teams.) It is obviously an important consideration, even ranking above knowing one's own abilities.

Having morally justified your response options you can plan accordingly for all the potential threats you might encounter. This is important when you review the types of threats out there. Not just terrorism but all of the everyday threats law enforcement encounters. Without having a predetermined and established combat mind-set, you may falter if faced with a Mumbai-style attack where you have multiple groups of adversaries attacking at the same time in different locations. What about an incident similar to the Beslan School assault that occurred in Russia on the first day of school in 2004. Chechen terrorists took over a local school full of children, eventually killing 385 people. These are some extreme examples, but the fact remains it can happen. In the United States we have had several high casualty events that have occurred at schools such as Sandy Hook and public events like the Pulse Night Club shooting.

Immediate action with deadly force by local officials could have saved numerous lives at any of these incidents. Indecision on the part of the first responders can be costly. Sun Tzu wrote, *In the midst of difficulties we are ready to seize an advantage, we may extricate ourselves from misfortune.* He understood that by preparing and training ahead of time you are more likely to prevail during an attack. We have also learned with active-shooter incidents that once a suspect is engaged by the police or an armed citizen his attention is diverted from the innocent victims, which in turn saves lives. This is where the combat mind-set comes in.

Terrorism is not going to go away. We will be faced with the threat of international terrorism from groups such as ISIS and al-Qaeda for quite some time, but we also have to take into account domestic terrorist groups and our homegrown lone wolf terrorists. Preparation will be the key to your survival in these high-risk situations. If we do not prepare and allow them to win and destroy our way of life, we will never get it back. Once destroyed, it is gone forever. Remember, *A kingdom that has once been destroyed can never come again into being; nor can the dead ever be brought back to life.*

Let's not see this happen on our watch.

Key Points

- Recognize the threat is here.

- Know your policies.

- Develop a winning combat mind-set.

Chapter 8   The Active Shooter Threat

> *Speed is of the essence in war. What is valued in war is a quick victory, not prolonged operations.*
>
> —Sun Tzu

What we today call an Active Shooter is nothing new. Law enforcement has been dealing with them for quite some time. It is just the way we are now recognizing the threat and how we respond to it that is different.

The standard operating procedure for years was to contain the situation the best we could and "wait for SWAT." We would attempt to negotiate and wait for an opportune time to make entry and mitigate the threat. This method took precious time and on occasion cost the lives of the innocent caught up in the situation. Patrol officers and those first on scene were sometimes willing to go in but were often held back by overly cautious administrators. This was said to have occurred in the infamous San Isidro McDonald's massacre in 1984 when the suspect entered the restaurant intent on killing people. The incident lasted for 77 minutes and cost the lives of 21 people until police sniper Chuck Foster was finally given authorization to end the threat. It is interesting to note that the delay was apparently owing to a commander who was en route to the scene and would not give his on scene personnel authorization to act. Sun Tzu wrote about situations like this when he said, *If fighting is sure to result in victory, then you must fight, even if the ruler forbids it.*

Even if officers in the past had been allowed to take action by their commanders, they were still often at a disadvantage from the beginning because of having had little, if any, training on how to properly handle these extremely high-risk situations.

An example of such an incident was the Texas Tower Shootings that occurred on August 1, 1966, when a sniper on the Tower killed 16 people and wounded an additional 32 people. The event was brought to a conclusion when two Austin Police

Officers, Ramiro Martinez and Jerry Day, entered the Tower and made contact with the shooter on the observation deck. With limited training, these officers successfully came up with a simple plan on their own, executed it and brought the episode to an end.

Incidents such as the Texas Tower Shooting actually led to the development of specialized teams to deal with these extremely dangerous situations. Unfortunately, the advanced training stayed within the teams and the average patrol officer, who would almost always be first on scene, received little or no additional training. They were simply told to set up a perimeter and "wait for SWAT."

In these types of situations, it takes an actual event that costs lives before administrators will think outside of the box and start spending time and valuable training dollars on procedures that deviate from the norm.

Most believe the paradigm shift for "active shooter training" came in 1999 after the attack by two students in Littleton, Colorado at Columbine High School. After the event, law enforcement was criticized for their initial response by everyone from the media to public officials. The toughest questions came from parents who wanted to know why their children died, and the officers who were sworn to protect them waited outside.

The following is a brief overview of the timeline of the Columbine Incident.

The first officer arrived on scene at 11:21 hrs, approximately two minutes after 911 calls reporting explosions on the campus. Other deputies arriving on scene exchanged gunfire with the suspects at 11:27 hrs. It is later determined that the majority of the 13 victims are killed and 24 others wounded prior the arrival of additional police officers between 11:29 and 11:36 hrs. This is approximately 15 minutes after the first officer arrived on scene. A standard response of containment was started when the two suspects were still actively moving throughout the school wounding and killing students and staff. At 11:49 hrs SWAT personnel arrive on scene and are ordered to make an immediate entry into the school, which does not actually occur until 11:52 hrs. SWAT team members are engaged by the suspects with gunfire during their approach and do not enter the building until 12:06 hrs. The two suspects then commit suicide at 12:08 hrs ending the standoff. A total of 40 minutes passed from the initial 911 call until police entered the building.

You cannot blame the officers on scene, because they did what they had been trained to do. They had responded to an extremely chaotic and fluid event, which included everyone from the initial patrol officer on scene, the first Patrol Sergeant to arrive and eventually to the SWAT Commander in charge of the operation to clear the building.

This incident made it clear that a new approach was needed when dealing with criminals who were still actively engaged in killing innocent victims. This included developing a new mind-set on dealing with these extremely active and fluid types of incidents.

Unfortunately for all the victims of "active shooters" over the years, Sun Tzu recognized thousands of years ago that a quick victory in all violent confrontations is more desirable than to prolong the operation. He wrote, *In war, let your great object be victory, not lengthy campaigns.* This was not a common thought among law enforcement for quite some time.

Columbine occurred at the same time our military was actively preparing and training for terrorist attacks. Many law enforcement trainers familiar with military tactics started to adopt these tactics to a police application for response to an active shooter or a terrorist attack. However, certain military tactics, such as clearing a room with a fragmentation grenade prior to making entry, would never be acceptable in a civilian law-enforcement environment. However, over the years, various military tactics and pieces of equipment such as armored vehicles and drones have been successfully adopted for the civilian law-enforcement world.

One of the biggest obstacles to overcome with patrol officers was to develop the winning combat mind-set that they needed and that they "were obligated" to enter the building, find, make contact and neutralize the threat while the situation is still extremely fluid and dangerous. Most SWAT officers during that time already had that mentality and were eager to go. Everyone else needed to catch up.

When my department started training for these situations, we trained our SWAT Team first in the most current tactics. The team was then used to train the rest of the department. We encountered resistance at first because some officers felt it wasn't their job to make the entry. My standard response to them was, "Excuse me. You are wearing a badge aren't you? It is *your* job."

All officers received the training, and some took to it right away. Others simply went through the motions to make it through the training day. They had no real sense of urgency to learn the tactics and take the training seriously. Then our department took a great leap forward and was one of the first in our county to start training with Simunition rounds. What an eye opening experience to conduct force-on-force training with live moving, thinking targets that shoot back compared to our standard bad guy paper targets. We set up a shoot-house in an abandoned warehouse and started training, eventually conducting countywide training sessions for other agencies. These sessions soon moved to off-site training locations such as schools and businesses in our local area. Some of the officers that did not take the training seriously in the beginning still did not, but the majority now understood the importance of covering your partner, moving from position to position and engaging with the enemy. As expected, our SWAT officers took to the training immediately, with others soon gaining a better appreciation of the officer safety tactics that would keep them safe.

One of the unintended benefits of conducting this training is that I soon realized who I wanted to go into a confrontation with and who were the ones better left outside. It was obvious some officers did not have and were unable to develop a warrior mindset. Some would joke around during training and treat it like we were playing cops and robbers. We even had one sergeant complain when he was hit by a Simunition round. He said it hurt too much. It took a while to explain to him that the training round hurt less than what the actual bullet would have felt like when it hit him. It also helped him better understand what "cover" meant. I think that experience helped him realize what we were trying to accomplish in our training. At least I hope it did.

Many of Sun Tzu's military principles can and should be used when dealing with active shooters. One of his principles addresses the fluid and sometimes unexpected nature of the incident itself. The shooter may not have carefully thought out his actions except to pick a target and bring a gun. Once the incident starts, chaos will set in for the suspect. This provides law enforcement with a distinct advantage if we have prepared in advance for these events. Sun Tzu stated, ***Take advantage of the enemy's unpreparedness, make your way by unexpected routes, and attack where he has made no precautions.***

Once the initial officers arrive on scene and form into a contact team, or a single officer decides to go alone, they need to use every bit of available information to locate the suspect. Options include quickly interviewing escaping civilians, accessing surveillance video if possible and, of course, the sounds of gunfire. Having a basic understanding of the layout of the location will greatly increase your chances of a successful operation.

This is why it is important to preplan and become familiar with locations in your jurisdiction. Sun Tzu also understood the importance of preplanning and obtaining information beforehand when he wrote, ***Thus, what enables the wise sovereign and the good general to strike and conquer, and achieve things beyond the reach of ordinary men, is foreknowledge.***

If you do not have time to prepare informational packets or target folders for potential target locations, at least try to do a walk-through and familiarize yourself with the location. If a detailed floor plan is not readily available, grab the fire-escape map and take it with you or take a photo of it with your cell phone. Try and approach the suspect from a direction he may not be anticipating. If he is planning for you to come in the front door, it may now be barricaded or he is just waiting to ambush you. Entering from a stairwell, a back service room or some other unexpected route may give you the advantage you need.

It is important to remember that if the suspect does stop somewhere to set up and the shooting has stopped, you are no longer in an "active shooter scenario." You now have a barricaded suspect with the possibility of hostages. Your tactics should now resort back to containment. Unless he begins shooting again, there is no need to endanger yourself or the hostages by making an entry and forcing the situation. Now is the time to wait for SWAT and the negotiators.

However, if he is still moving and shooting you need to keep the pressure on. Sun Tzu states, ***Keep him under strain and wear him down.*** Eventually he will make a mistake and expose himself so you can "end the threat." There is another of Sun Tzu's principles that is relevant here. He writes, ***If the enemy leaves the door open, you must rush in.***

The active shooter scenario also brought out the need for officers to be armed with sufficient firepower to deal with a multitude of threats, which became crystal clear to the law enforcement community in 1997 during the North Hollywood Bank Robbery. Patrol officers responding with 9 mm handguns, .38 cal. revolvers and shotguns were dealing with suspects covered in body armor firing fully automatic assault rifles.

Although this scenario does not happen every day, the fact remains you cannot predict for certainty where or when it will happen. Therefore you must be prepared. By recognizing the potential threat, departments began to authorize officers to carry "patrol rifles." These rifles had been common in rural communities for years, but administrators in urban areas did not want to see them in Downtown USA. They were deemed to be "too militaristic" and "too powerful."

These rifles are now a common fixture in most cities and should be readily available to all qualified officers. To my mind, they are the weapon of choice when dealing with an active shooter, or for any other high-risk incident for that matter. With a patrol rifle you have greater penetration ability for suspects wearing body armor and you can hit your targets at greater distances. Remember, you are most likely going to encounter these shooters in places like schools with long hallways, large parking lots, big industrial businesses, other workplace environments and the occasional "gun free zone." You should ask yourself, are you really that good with your handgun?

When preparing for active shooter scenarios you have to do the following. Develop your winning combat mind-set, prepare in advance and train, train, train. This will help you survive one of the most dangerous situations you might be called upon to handle.

Sun Tzu understood the importance of preparation and training and how it assists the soldier in battle. Sun Tzu writes, ***Hence the experienced soldier, once in motion, is never bewildered; once he has broken camp, he is never at a loss.*** This is what it will take to survive an active shooter situation.

Key Points

- Develop a winning combat mind-set.

- Do the unexpected and take the fight to the suspect.

- Prepare as much in advance as possible.

- Utilize the most effective weapon—usually a Patrol Rifle.

Chapter 9   Special Response Teams

> *Their aim must be to take all under heaven*
> *intact through strategic superiority.*
>   —Sun Tzu

A common misperception held by many is that a Special Weapons and Tactics Team (SWAT) is just a bunch of gung-ho prior military folks who only want to go out and storm buildings and shoot the bad guys. Thanks to Hollywood and faulty media coverage, this misconception continues today. Unfortunately, it is a reality that a gung-ho team is formed on occasion with a narrow mission profile and the people selected for the team make it because of the "good ole boy network." These situations are what keeps the gung-ho SWAT stereotype going, especially in the media. Fortunately, the majority of modern SWAT Teams are highly trained professionals who no longer fit that stereotype. Most teams now adhere to a very high level of state and national standards.

Before SWAT Teams were officially formed in the late 1960s, departments did not have a formalized way of handling high-risk situations. They may have resorted to tapping the skills of some military veterans and sending them into harm's way with little or no training (and even fewer resources). This approach did not always end well.

After high-profile incidents such has the Texas Tower Shooting, the Watts Riots and the Black Panther Shootouts in Los Angeles it was clear there was a need for specialized teams to handle these high-risk incidents.

The Los Angeles Police Department was one of the first to organize a team after a proposal by then Det. Daryl Gates (later Chief Gates) was approved.

Today's modern SWAT teams have grown since the 1960s. They are known by several different names to include Special Response Team (SRT), Emergency Response Team (ERT), Mobile Emergency Response Group and Equipment (MERGE) and the

FBI's Hostage Rescue Team, but they all do essentially the same job.

The California Peace Officers Standards and Training (POST) defines a SWAT Team as "any designated group of law enforcement officers who are selected, trained, and equipped to work as a coordinated team to resolve critical incidents that are so hazardous, complex, or unusual that they may exceed the capabilities of first responders or investigative units." Members of these teams are some of the more highly motivated officers within a department that enjoy training and challenging themselves to go above and beyond what they encounter in normal police work. They like working together where individualism is not encouraged. They like trusting themselves to their partners in high-risk situations. They are the ones who are willing to train on their own and keep themselves in great physical shape. They are the ones that real SWAT Teams are made of.

Sun Tzu recognized that having a specialized unit of good fighting men is important to be decisive on the battlefield. He recognized that they could carry the fight and win the battle when set in motion. Sun Tzu writes, *Thus the energy developed by good fighting men is as the momentum of a round stone rolled down a mountain thousands of feet in height.*

I consider it an honor that I was selected to be a member of my department's SWAT Team. The selection process was hard and there were always several candidates attempting to get a slot. Once I was selected and completed Basic SWAT training, like everyone else, I had a great sense of pride pinning on my SWAT pin.

However, with the selection came several full-time responsibilities that I had to be prepared for. The first one is the time commitment. In addition to all of the individual training time that goes with the position, you have to be prepared for the unplanned callout. Over the years, I have missed many family events that can never be replaced because some suspect had no regard for my personal schedule and had barricaded himself in a building or committed some other violent crime.

The second responsibility is that you suddenly become the tactical expert for the rest of your patrol shift. Many patrol supervisors do not have any background with SWAT and when faced with a situation that could be considered "tactical," they will rely on your newfound expertise, even if you have been on the team for only a few weeks. It is the same principle that occurs to new detectives. Somehow, by wearing a suit, you are suddenly smarter than the average patrol officer. The same thing happens when you put on your tactical vest and helmet. You will be called on to give advice and make decisions, but the one thing of consequence is that as a SWAT operator your decisions can literally be life and death. Therefore, you had better take your position on the team extremely seriously and train that way.

The goal of every SWAT Team is to resolve high-risk situations without anyone getting hurt, which this includes everyone involved from the innocent bystander, the victims, you and the other officers at the scene and even the suspect. This is not always possible because we cannot control every possible factor during the event. We are dealing with unpredictable, irrational and highly emotional situations. On occasion, we may even deal with a highly intelligent suspect who wants nothing more than to "outsmart" the police. Because of this, we need to prepare for every possible contingency to contain and control the situation. We must also be ready and able to react with the appropriate level of force to end the situation if it becomes deadly to anyone involved.

In an effort to better prepare for all of these contingencies, Sun Tzu's entire work should be read by SWAT commanders, team leaders and operators. His work was obviously intended for the military and warfare, and this is why it is especially important for SWAT operators and commanders to be familiar with Sun Tzu's principles, because when a SWAT Team is deployed, the team is in fact engaged in a "war."

All of Sun Tzu's principles can be applied in a SWAT situation. The main difference between the military and law enforcement are the rules of engagement we have to work under. There is also no acceptable or anticipated lose category in police work.

Commanders and team leaders must understand the capabilities of their team and understand the threat they are going up against. In this way, they can properly deploy their troops, gather intelligence and bring the situation to a close.

Sun Tzu provides us with a guide for predicting victory during any situation using the following five criteria.

There are 5 circumstances in which victory may be predicted.

He who knows when he can fight and
when he cannot will be victorious.

He who understands how to use both large and
small forces will be victorious.

He whose ranks are united in purpose will be victorious.

He who is prudent and lies in wait for an enemy who is not,
will be victorious.

He whose generals are able and not interfered with
by the sovereign will be victorious.

—Sun Tzu

If these five principles are adhered to in the planning phase and throughout the operation, your chances of success will be greatly enhanced. Now, let's take a closer look at these circumstances.

In the first circumstance SWAT operators must know if they are prepared to contact the suspect and be prepared for a potential fight. If you are not prepared and you engage with the suspect, there is a chance you will not be successful in your operation. It is important for your unit, from the commander to the operators, that you conduct a self-analysis and honestly critique your capabilities. Have you trained for the mission you are about to undertake? Do you have the resources you need? Are you mentally ready? You have to be honest with yourself because if you are not ready, victory will not be yours.

Team leaders and supervisors must be well versed about team movements and techniques on where to position their team members to achieve maximum benefit. This is covered in the second circumstance. Everyone involved needs to have overall comprehensive and cohesive understanding of the terrain in which they are operating. Without a good overall understanding of tactics and the capacity to anticipate the moves of your opponent, the likelihood of success is greatly diminished, because the suspect will have the advantage.

In the third circumstance, Sun Tzu talks about why all Team Members, from Commanders to Operators, must believe in the operation and understand their roles. If there is confusion or an unwillingness to carry out an order, the mission is lost. If everyone is motivated and on the same page the mission is on the road to success. A team with low esprit de corps will not function properly. The motivation level to seek and secure success must be at a high point. This all comes from proper training and having a clear focus on what the goal is.

Sun Tzu also writes about how Team members must be patient during the operation and not prone to rush the event unnecessarily. We have time on our side unless the suspect pushes the pace such as in an active shooter incident. Once the suspect starts to rush, he will begin to make mistakes, which can be exploited by Team members who have planned and are prepared. Again, proper planning and training ahead of time will ensure that each team member knows their roles and what is expected of them. Such assurance will prevent a feeling of panic, which can lead to rushing things and eventual disaster.

And finally, the team should be allowed to work on its own. After given its mission and objective, outside influences on the team should be avoided at all costs. The job of the Department's Administration and Team Commanders is to set policies and goals, not how to actually go about accomplishing the mission. Outside command staff who are not versed on the exact capabilities of the SWAT Team will often have unrealistic expectations of what the team can do. Team Commanders and Team Leaders must be willing to set the standard for the team and control the operation free of outside influences. They also need to stand up to administrators and set them straight when they are asked to accomplish something the team cannot deliver

With these five principles in mind, the majority of SWAT operations, along with other tactical situations, will end successfully because the team has prepared and is ready.

Commanders will be able to predict the outcome of high risk encounters using another set of principles that Sun Tzu laid out in *The Art of War*:

By means of these 7 elements, I can forecast victory or defeat.

1. *Which sovereign possesses greater moral influence*
2. *Which commander is more capable*
3. *Which side holds more favorable conditions in weather and terrain*
4. *On which side are decrees better implemented*
5. *Which side is superior in arms*
6. *On which side are officers and men better trained.*
7. *Which side is stricter and more impartial in meting out rewards and punishments.*

If the sovereign heeds these stratagems of mine and acts upon them, he will surely win the war, and I shall, therefore stay with him. If the sovereign neither heeds nor acts upon them, he will certainly suffer defeat, and I shall leave.
—Sun Tzu

Sun Tzu used these criteria to assess commanders when he was making his decision on whether to follow and support them or not. These seven criteria should also be used to evaluate your adversary and then compare them with the responses from your own command staff. This is a great tool to use for a self-analysis to see if you are as prepared as you think you are.

The seven criteria are fairly self-explanatory. However, the definition of "moral influence" in the first example is one item I think needs to be clarified. I believe Sun Tzu used this term when determining the difference between right and wrong and good or bad and who possess the greater amount of Integrity. The sovereign on the right side will have a greater degree of "moral influence" and, therefore, will be more likely to prevail.

If the answers to each set of circumstances and principles are all in favor of the commander and he plans accordingly, victory will be his. Modern-day SWAT Commanders, or any officer faced with a high-risk situation should also apply these elements when deciding on a plan of action. They should take the time to assess each category and see what side they are on. To assure success, the situation must be modified if there are deficiencies to providing the greatest chance of accomplishing your goal.

Sun Tzu understood how important it was to study your enemy. But he also understood how important it is to understand yourself and what you are capable of. Sun Tzu wrote, *If you know the enemy and know yourself, you need not fear the result of hundred battles. If you know yourself but not the enemy, for every victory gained you will also suffer a defeat. If you know neither the enemy nor yourself, you will succumb in every battle.*

By following all of these principles that Sun Tzu laid out, the SWAT Commander and his Team are able to fulfill their primary mission, which is the Sun Tzu maxim, *In the practical art of war, the best thing of all is to take the enemy's country whole and intact.*

Sun Tzu's work should be a part of every SWAT Operator's playbook. A good understanding of his principle's will lead to a positive outcome in most every situation.

Key Points

- Be prepared for the extra responsibility.

- All SWAT operators should be aware of Sun Tzu's Principles.

- Believe in the mission.

- Understand what is meant by "moral Influence."

- Know your enemy and know yourself.

Chapter 10   The Sniper

> *Foreknowledge must be obtained from men who know the enemy situation.*
>
> —Sun Tzu

OK. I admit this chapter is included because I am biased toward police snipers and, being this is my first book, I have decided to indulge myself. The reason for my bias is that I was one of our department's SWAT snipers beginning in 2001 (retiring in 2016). However, once I decided to include a specific chapter dealing with snipers, I found several Sun Tzu maxims that apply to this topic.

During my time in the military I was never assigned or trained as a military sniper, but I have always had a fascination with the assignment. I had heard the heroic stories of military snipers during the Vietnam War such as Chuck Mahwinney and Carlos Hathcock. Their true stories are the stuff of legends. There are several others that have stood out in all of our previous conflicts. They include snipers such as Herbert McBride from World War One. In World War Two our Finnish allies had Simo Hayha who had 542 confirmed kills. His career ended when he was shot in the head but survived to live a long life. I encourage anyone interested in becoming a sniper, whether military or police to read the stories of these men (and women). And thanks to men like Navy Seal Chris Kyle and Canadian Sniper Craig Harrison, we have a whole new generation of snipers to learn from.

I realized early on in my police career that the role of a law-enforcement sniper (or designated marksman for the politically correct) is much more than being an expert marksman. He has the responsibility, especially in a crisis situation, to provide intelligence to the on-scene tactical commander who may not be in a position to see what is going on for himself. It can then become the sniper's responsibility to intervene with a well-aimed precision shot that does not have the option to miss. That one shot can bring a barricaded hostage situation or other violent encounter in which lives are at stake to an end. The sniper also needs to work in conjunction with the other elements of the SWAT Team to provide over-watch when they are moving in hostile and unfriendly territory. The team needs to trust that the sniper can make the shot and he needs to communicate effectively with the team to ensure that everyone is safe.

Sun Tzu recognized the need for commanders to obtain as much information as possible on the enemy before he commits his troops and then obtain constant updates to ensure the mission is going as planned. Knowing that no plan stays the same once in motion, the need for updates is crucial. This is why Sun Tzu wrote about obtaining "foreknowledge." This knowledge can come from many sources including spies, which Sun Tzu also wrote about extensively in his book. (In modern law enforcement we might call them Confidential Informants.) However, once the operation is underway, the commander needs to be kept updated of any and all changes. These updates should include information on suspect description and location, on fortifications that may have been made, on outside resources that have arrived to help the suspect, on changes in the approach route for the good guys, and so on. All of this information can be obtained from a properly trained sniper that is given the time and resources to move into an advantageous position and set up. Sun Tzu wrote of this when he said, *By discovering the enemy's dispositions and remaining invisible ourselves, we can keep our forces concentrated, while the enemy must be divided.*

Commanders have to be well trained on the capabilities of their snipers and know what they can and cannot do. Contrary to popular belief, snipers are not Superheroes that can suddenly materialize in the proper position at the snap of a finger. If they are forced to rush into a position they may give themselves and their location away, which would most likely compromise the mission.

To better blend in with the environment in which they will be working, many snipers rely on camouflage and use what is called a Guille Suit. The suit is actually three-dimensional camouflage that enables the sniper to blend in with the surroundings in a rural environment (although it does not always work as well in an urban setting). The use of such suits and proper camouflage follows Sun Tzu's principle, *All warfare is based on deception.* For operations in an urban setting, snipers should rely more on concealment and hiding in the shadows. It is important that deployed snipers remain unseen to complete their mission.

Once a sniper is in position, Sun Tzu gave some principles to watch for in Chapter 9—The Army on the March in his book, *The Art of War*, when an army is preparing to or actually on the move. Several of these principles apply to what a modern law-enforcement sniper may look for when observing a suspect. All of these principles should be studied, but here are three of particular importance.

Sun Tzu states, **When there is much running about and the soldiers fall into ranks, it means the critical moment has come.** This would be an important observation if a suspect threatens to commit a certain act, like execute a hostage, at a predetermined time. If he starts "running about" arranging things to commit such an act, the tactical commander should be made aware of this to initiate a rescue or have the sniper eliminate the threat.

Another of Sun Tzu's principles states, **When the soldiers stand leaning on their spears, they are faint from want of food.** When your adversary is tired and hungry, they will not be as alert, which would be an ideal time to initiate an assault. If the suspects are well-supplied and rested, other plans may be needed and the operation will need to be prolonged.

Military snipers may also notice when enemy forces are overworked and exhausted. This is an advantageous time for a possible assault. Sun Tzu recognized this and wrote, **If the enemy see an advantage to be gained and makes no effort to secure it, the soldiers are exhausted.**

These are but three of the tenets that Sun Tzu wrote about that apply when observing the enemy. Every sniper studies these principles already in one way or another and is aware of their importance, but it is interesting to see how it was written about 2,500 years ago and is still relevant today.

Snipers are also more likely than not to be your more-motivated SWAT Operators when it comes to training and maintaining their skills. On top of their regular weapons qualifications, extra training time needs to be allocated for the sniper. The sniper needs to master several skills to include range and wind estimation, field craft and communication skills. He must also be in top physical shape to ensure he can handle a prolonged situation. Remember that the sniper must plan for several contingencies and, therefore, must bring a substantial amount of equipment with him the first time. He won't have the luxury of going back for more.

We must understand there is a distinct difference between a marksman and a sniper. Almost anyone with a little training and a good rifle system can fire a tight shot group from the prone position at 100 yards on a static range. The true sniper has trained to make that one precision shot while under extreme stress when the target might be moving and holding a hostage at an unknown distance. The sniper also may be required to make the shot immediately after arriving on scene, or after several hours of watching and waiting for the opportune moment. The sniper must also be smart enough to know when not to shoot.

Weapon and equipment maintenance is also a priority for a sniper because the weapon system cannot fail and, once he deploys, there is usually no chance for resupply. Snipers must plan ahead and be prepared for almost any situation. I believe police snipers should bring enough supplies to last for at least 8 hours, which include water and food in an urban environment. Of course, this all depends on your particular situation and environment. In an extreme rural setting you might need supplies to last several days.

On my team, as in most, the snipers need to be proficient in all aspects of SWAT operations so they know the roles of all the various operators. On occasion, when I was not deployed as a sniper, I found myself in the stack going in with the team. Snipers need to understand the team's tactics to provide any support the team may need and to provide effective overwatch during the operation. In addition, snipers need to work independently and with little supervision. Most snipers usually work in pairs, with one partner acting as the sniper and the other the spotter. However, this does not always happen, and snipers can be forced to deploy alone depending on the developing situation.

Officers trained as snipers have to make decisions on their own that could affect the entire operation, which is especially true when the decision involves employing deadly force. I always thought it was strange that tactical commanders would assume control of the sniper at the last minute and allow them to fire only with a "Green Light." Snipers should understand their parameters and be given some direction, but they should also be trusted to fire when they feel it is appropriate. A new recruit fresh out of the Academy does not have to wait for permission to fire his weapon. You would think that a highly trained SWAT operator assigned to be a sniper would know when to shoot. This is where realistic training scenarios are essential for the police sniper and ensure they are experts in the Use of Force. Good communication is essential among the Commander, Team Leaders and Sniper so that everyone is on the same page. The snipers need to train outside of the box and prepare themselves for the unexpected. All of this training will lead to an increased amount of trust by everyone on the team and on what the sniper can and cannot do for them.

Snipers in the military and in police work are a rare breed. Not everyone can or wants to be a sniper, but for those who do and can become proficient in the trade, having a good understanding of Sun Tzu's principles will be of utmost value. I believe with the proper training, equipment and mind-set any soldier or officer can survive on today's modern battlefield. This is especially true for snipers. Sun Tzu understood this when he wrote, *Hence the skillful fighter puts himself into a position which makes defeat impossible, and does not miss the moment for defeating the enemy.*

Key Points

- Obtain as much information as possible beforehand.

- Develop trust with your teammates.

- Train outside of the box.

- Maintain exceptional weapon proficiency.

Part Two

PREPARATION

Chapter 11   The Need for Training

> *The art of war teaches us to rely not on the likelihood of the enemy's not coming, but on our own readiness to receive him.*
> —Sun Tzu

I have always been a firm believer that the need for thorough preparation and training is especially important in law enforcement when working on the streets or, for that matter, any other assignment. Encountering a violent offender is not the time to start thinking about what your plan is, or to start wishing you had trained more with your handgun or had practiced your defensive tactics on a more regular basis. Worse yet, it is not the time to wish you had more luck on your side.

The average offender does not have your level of professional training, but he is probably just as determined to accomplish his goal as you are, whether that is to just get away from you or to take you out of the picture. (Hopefully, he is not more determined than you.) The person you are dealing with may have years of non-professional training derived from such places as prison, county jails or from just living on the streets. The training he has received may not have been formalized, but it can be just has effective if he applies it in the way it was intended.

On rare occasions you may also go up against a person with extensive professional training. Look at the chaos a single rogue police officer with military training caused in Southern California in February 2013.

In our profession, we have to remember there is always a chance we are not going home at the end of the shift. In fact, in 2015, 124 officers did not. We all go to work every day facing that possibility, and I, for one, want to do everything I can to shift the odds of going home in my favor. The way to do that is to train.

Sun Tzu understood that a soldier cannot go into battle simply hoping the enemy does not show up. He has to prepare that the enemy is coming with everything he has. We also have to assume the same thing, because it is up to us as individuals to ultimately be responsible for ourselves. We cannot rely solely on our training managers and department administrators to provide us with all of the additional training we need. Time restraints and budget issues greatly affect what can be provided to us by our organizations. Therefore, we need to better ourselves whenever we can, which means on our own time and at our own expense.

Case law such as *City of Canton v. Harris* (Lack of Proper Training) and *Popow v. City of Margate* (Lack of Realistic Training) set standards for departments to follow about training. They also gave us a definition of "negligent training." To overcome shortcomings of the training, officers who are serious about improving their individual skills and increasing their odds of survival will need to seek out their own supplemental training.

The quote from Sun Tzu at the top of this chapter actually continues, ... ***not on the chance of his not attacking, but rather on the fact that we have made our position unassailable.*** We must prepare ourselves to survive and become "unassailable" by obtaining all the necessary training available and then maintaining our proficiency in those skills.

When I say "train," it is not only going to training classes and doing the minimum to pass. It means that you have to train as if your life and others you care about depends on it, because it does. I am always amazed at the number of officers that take a casual approach to their officer safety training. Some are actually upset about being there. When you train you should push yourself outside of your comfort zone so you can improve your skills and know your capabilities. When firearms training may save your life, why would you practice it only quarterly (and sometimes only once a year) to merely achieve an average or passing score? Some officers still go to the range only when their departments mandate it. Usually, these are the officers that train only because they are ordered to. Their Training Sergeant has to send them because it is required department or state mandatory training. Well, it is mandatory for a reason.

Officers and training managers need to understand the difference between Qualifications and Training. When you run someone through a Qualification Course they receive a Pass / Fail score. This type of course is simply a liability-mitigation tool to show that an officer has met a set of minimum standards. It is not comprehensive training sessions that expose the officer to new ideas and concepts.

The majority of officer safety-training courses are designed to teach successful principles that have been learned the hard way, which usually means that someone has lost his or her life or was seriously injured because of a mistake. We learn what went wrong in these incidents and how to fix them so they don't happen again.

A good example of such an incident occurred on April 6, 1970, to four California Highway Patrol Officers. The event changed the way law enforcement officers were trained and simply became known as The Newhall Incident. It is the subject of the Case Study for this chapter.

It is worth repeating here that it is imperative we take training seriously because our lives and those of our partners may very well depend on it. A famous saying often attributed to General George S. Patton and heard repeatedly in military training applies here, "It is better to sweat in training than bleed in battle." This is definitely something worth remembering.

Once we have learned something new we need to maintain a proficient level in whatever skill it is. All physical skills, such as defensive tactics, emergency vehicle operations and weapons expertise, are perishable and must be sustained. Going back to the basics regarding any skill and solidifying the fundamentals will always help us to improve. That is why state agencies like the California Peace Officers Standards in Training (POST) mandate periodic training for all perishable skills.

It is important to realize that what we learn in the safety of the classroom, a padded mat room or on a static firing range will not always translate to the stressful environment of a deadly force encounter on the streets. This is why we need to train outside of our comfort zone. We need to push ourselves. The stress of real-life situations is hard to replicate in training, but we need to approach it as closely as possible.

When experiencing a high-stress situation, especially for the first time, your blood pressure will increase to levels close to 145 BPM or higher, which causes several reactions in your body, including auditory exclusion, focused tunnel vision and the inability to complete complex motor skills. It will also slow reaction times, especially if you have to choose between several different options to complete a task. Simplicity and limiting yourself to just a few options will benefit you in these high-risk situations. Another must-read on this topic is the excellent book, *Sharpening the Warrior's Edge*, by Bruce Siddle (1995). Siddle explains in detail how stress affects you and provides insights on how to overcome these limitations and develop your training to meet these needs.

As we learn, it is important to understand the mental process we go through before we know we are competent in a particular task. Let us take a moment and look at the four levels of learning that we experience.

The first level is Unconscious Incompetence, which is where it all begins for a student who needs to learn something that he does not know he needs to learn. He does not have a clue of what is expected of him and may be completely unfamiliar with the topic. This is a common occurrence for law enforcement recruits who may not have any idea what they are getting into and what is expected of them when they start the Academy.

The second level is Conscious Incompetence. At this point the student is aware of what is expected of him but is unaware of how to proceed. He may have seen the completed objective in practice but has no idea of how to get there. This is when our Recruit looks at the Academy curriculum and is told what he or she needs to do to graduate but does not know how to get there without guidance.

The third level is Conscious Competence. At this juncture, the student or recruit has received some training on how to reach his objective. He may even be able to do it but still needs practice to perfect the move or skill. He may need to talk himself through each step. I would say this is about where the recruit will be at or just after graduation from the Academy. He knows enough to pass the tests, but has he really mastered everything?

The fourth and final level is Unconscious Competence. At this stage the skill becomes second nature and you can perform it without concentrated thought. To get to this level, multiple repetitions of the skill are required along with a period of continued sustainment training. Once you enter level 4 you have actually learned something. Most officers agree this stage occurs for the recruit around the five-year mark after leaving the Academy and when his skills have been used repeatedly.

If you ever get a chance to watch a professional sports team practice, you will notice they take the time to brush up on their basics on a regular basis. Kyle McLaren, who played for 12 years in the NHL for the Bruins and Sharks (and was known for his vicious hip check), told me, "Mastering the basics played an important role in everything we practiced. We always spent time on the fundamentals."

Whether it is hockey players doing basic stick-to-stick passes or football players running simple post patterns, it all comes back to basics. In law enforcement, if you cannot draw your weapon from the holster in a smooth and efficient manner, it does not matter how well or fast you can conduct a tactical speed reload. And then if you do get the weapon out, you still need a smooth steady trigger pull and proper sight alignment to deliver effective rounds on your target. These are all the basics you learned in Firearms 101 at the Academy, and they will always apply.

Too often, officers want to skip the basics and spend all their time trying to master a high-speed technique and do it as fast as they can; which is great, but if you are not hitting your target consistently every time you do the drill, you are going too fast. I see this inclination a lot when I teach civilian firearms classes. Students want to shoot like the guys in the movies and do all the high-speed stuff. Then, when they miss, they cannot figure out why. I relate a quote to them that was attributed to Wyatt Earp, famous for the gunfight at the OK Corral, who said, "Smooth is fast. Fast is smooth." To get smooth, learn the basics. To get fast, master the basics and get smooth.

I try to go to all the training courses I can for a full exposure to a wide variety of tactics and techniques. I may not always incorporate what I learn in these classes into my everyday activities, but I'll try it during class and evaluate it. There have been several times when I started a class and heard what the instructor had planned and thought to myself, "This is crap. I'll never use it." Well, more times than not, I learned why the instructor taught what he taught and why and then agreed that the technique had some merit. Of course, there were also times when my initial assessment was correct. This does not mean I disregard the technique completely. It may not have worked for me, but it probably works for someone somewhere, and you should be aware of it. It is also important to be aware of unsafe tactics being taught so you can try and stop them when they are encountered in other venues. The Internet is a good place to find these unsafe and unusual tactics.

I use a simple checklist to evaluate techniques to decide if I will use them and potentially teach them in my classes. The first criteria I use is simplicity, because I feel it is the most important. I ask, is the technique simple enough that it can be taught and then recalled in a moment of crisis? We all fall back to our training when stressed; if, in the heat of the moment, we have to hesitate to recall a multistep process, we are sure to fail.

My second evaluation criteria asks, Does the technique make sense? If it does not, then I won't believe in it and, therefore, I won't seriously train for it. For example, I have seen various techniques to conduct a tactical reload of a rifle. I've tried them all, and I have stuck with the ones that have made sense to me. They all will get your rifle reloaded, but some take too long and others take your attention away from the threat. Others simply add too many unnecessary steps. Evaluate everything and decide what makes sense for you.

Finally, my third criteria is, Does it work in the real world? Is the technique street proven? I enjoy taking classes from instructors who are legitimate professionals and can truly say, "Been there. Done that." These are instructors who I will more than likely trust when they tell me the technique worked for them and others in combat or on the streets. However, I have been to several self-defense classes where a knife-defense technique or something similar was taught and the instructor had to make sure the "attacker" moved in a prearranged way and at a certain speed while demonstrating the technique. This is great for demonstration purposes and is the way a new technique should be taught, but rarely did the instructor invite a full-speed, unplanned attack so he could demonstrate that the technique actually works in a real-world application. On the occasion when a student would pick up the pace the instructor would usually tell the student to stop or slow down and then find an excuse to move on to something else. If your instructor is unwilling to demonstrate a technique at full speed, or if the technique does not appear when sparring, it is probably not worth learning. At least it is not worth spending too much time on.

Another important aspect of training that not all officers take seriously is scenario role-playing. I'll admit that I do not always enjoy participating in scenarios because they are sometimes unrealistic, and it is hard to "notionalize" what is going on. However, if the scenario is set up well, there is no better training around to test your skills. This type of training is the best way to raise your students' stress levels and heart rates to see how they will respond. I have been fortunate enough to participate as a SWAT Team member and as an Assistant Team Leader several times in an event called Urban Shield sponsored by the Alameda County Sheriff's Office. Urban Shield is a 48-hour nonstop series of 36 scenarios that are designed to test SWAT Team operators in a variety of stressful situations. The scenarios are all well-planned and staffed and provide a very realistic training opportunity. The manpower and planning involved in running an Urban Shield event, which covers over four counties in the San Francisco Bay Area, would be overwhelming for most agencies or communities. It takes almost a year to coordinate everything to put it on. The event also allows teams from around the world to participate. The event is now being duplicated in other big cities like Dallas and Boston.

In addition to Urban Shield I have also participated in a SWAT Training competition called Best in the West sponsored by the Santa Clara County Sheriff's Office. This event encompasses seven stations in which a six-person tactical team competes. Some of the events involve vehicle and building assaults, sniper engagements, physical fitness tests and advanced marksmanship skills. Best in the West is a great training event if you go for the right reasons. You need to realize that it is predominantly a shooting and marksmanship scored event and presents shooters with stressful individual and team situations. The danger with these competitions is that when the event is scored and timed, sound tactical doctrine sometimes goes right out the window in the interest of getting a better score. I would encourage you to participate in any competition you can such as this, but keep in mind what you are planning on getting out of it.

Not all officers can participate in large-scale events such as these. However, with a little work, you can organize a local event for your department or just for a small group of officers. These events can be a simple shooting competition or a series of full-blown scenarios.

If you are organizing your own training and plan to introduce force-on-force or other stress-inducing techniques, I strongly encourage you to read Ken Murray's book, *Training at the Speed of Life*. He is a cofounder of Simunitions and his book will help you set up safe and effective simulation training. This is beneficial because it will push you to your limits and test your skills.

Another great way to challenge yourself and test your skills is by using an interactive-training simulator. This is a luxury item that most smaller agencies cannot afford, but if you are lucky enough to have access to one, open it up for officers to train on. Some of the programs offer straight marksmanship training, where others can put an officer in a highly realistic training environment.

The danger with simulators is when the training is not taken seriously and the instructor runs the scenarios like a giant video game. The scenarios must be treated seriously and the officers should be challenged to justify their actions. They need to be able to explain why they did or did not fire their weapons. Some trainers will actually have officers write reports after a scenario to see how much information they can recall from the incident.

However, even if you cannot participate in such training events, you can still conduct training scenarios every time you are on patrol or have some down time. The power of conducting mental role-playing and running a scenario through your head is invaluable. Athletes do it all the time. They visualize themselves running the perfect pattern and catching the ball in the end zone or shooting the perfect slap shot past the goalie with only seconds left in the game. They may not get the chance to do these activities in every game, but if and when they do, they have at least done it before a thousand times in their heads. This technique of mental role-playing will help you build your response plan and lower your reaction times to various events that may not be common to you.

You can use these techniques while driving around on patrol. For example, when you drive past your local convenience store imagine you see the clerk being held-up at gunpoint. What would you do? How would you call it in on the radio? Where would you set up and where would you send responding units? Evaluate your answers and see if anything better comes up. What could go wrong with your plan? How could you improve? These are things to think about before the actual call comes out. Preplan and be prepared.

Another way to train and evaluate yourself is by using mental debriefings on calls you have just left that went well and ask yourself, "What if it went bad?" Change the scenario and ask what if questions at different points as you review your call. Were you prepared for your what ifs? If not, what could you have done better? You can do this by yourself or with your partner. Doing After Action Reports (AARs) or debriefings are an invaluable way to better yourself. Good tactical team leaders will always conduct a formal debriefing (also known as a Hot Wash) with the team after an operation. This is where everyone can get (and give) honest feedback to correct deficiencies and reinforce the positive.

Your training is an important part of your overall survival package and should not be taken lightly. Proper training will limit potential mistakes that could turn your battle in favor of the enemy. Sun Tzu wrote about this when he stated, *He wins his battles by making no mistakes. Making no mistakes is what establishes the certainty of victory.*

Whenever possible try and find ways to improve yourself so you can avoid making the same mistakes so many others have made in the past. I do not know who first said this but it is vitally important to remember that when the situation becomes critical, "We do not rise to the level of our expectations, we drop to the level of our training."

Make sure your drop is not too far.

Key Points

- Train as if your life depends on it.

- Evaluate the training you receive.

- Conduct scenarios and rehearsals.

- Be Prepared.

Case Study
The Newhall Incident

The Newhall Incident occurred in Southern California in an unincorporated area of Los Angeles County on April 6, 1970. This incident brought to bear many concerns about the way officers are trained and changed firearms training forever.

The incident started at approximately midnight when California Highway Patrol Officers Roger Gore and Walter Frago initiated a traffic stop on a vehicle that had been involved in a weapon-brandishing case earlier in the evening. The driver of the suspect vehicle complied with officers' commands and exited his vehicle and walked to the front of the CHP cruiser where he was patted down by Officer Gore. Officer Frago was standing by on the passenger side of the cruiser holding a shotgun at port arms. Officer Frago started to walk with the shotgun toward the suspect vehicle to see why the passenger was not exiting as he was instructed. However, the passenger suddenly exited his vehicle, produced a handgun and shot Officer Frago twice with two .357 Magnum rounds, which killed the officer. The first suspect simultaneously produced a handgun from his waist band and shot Officer Gore twice at point blank range, mortally wounding him.

While this was occurring a second CHP unit containing Officers Pence and Alleyn arrived on scene and was immediately fired upon by the two suspects. Officer Alleyn returned fire with his Remington 870 shotgun at the suspects. He fired so fast that he accidently ejected a live round in the process. A single shotgun pellet struck one of the suspects in the forehead, but it did not penetrate his skull and caused only a minor wound. Now with an empty shotgun, the officer opened fire with his .357 Magnum revolver but hit neither suspect. One of the suspects returned fire with a sawed-off shotgun and struck Officer Alleyn with several rounds of 00 buckshot, which inflicted fatal wounds.

During this time, a private citizen with military experience picked up the loaded shotgun that Officer Frago had dropped when he was shot and tried to engaged the suspects. The citizen did not realize the shotgun had not been fired and tried to cycle the weapon. While doing so he accidently fired the weapon, which startled him, causing him to drop it. He then grabbed the revolver from the officer's duty holster.

While this was going on, Officer Pence fired all six rounds from his revolver at the suspects and missed. He was then struck in the chest and in both legs from gunfire by the suspects and fell to the ground. While attempting to reload his revolver he was approached by a suspect from behind and shot in the back of the head.

The citizen now realized the situation was hopeless and fled the scene to seek cover in a nearby ditch. As the suspects were fleeing the scene, they exchanged gunfire with a third CHP unit that had arrived on scene and were able to escape on foot into the dark, traveling in separate directions.

One of the suspects was later arrested after being involved in a shootout with an armed citizen while trying to break into his camper. When he was out of ammunition he surrendered to the police without incident.

The second suspect broke into a house and took hostages. He later released the hostage but refused to surrender. The police eventually pumped tear gas into the house and made entry. When the police made entry, the suspect killed himself with a CHP shotgun that he had taken from the initial scene.

Because of this tragic incident several training issues were discovered in the aftermath. The officers were not issued speed loaders and attempted to load one round at a time during the firefight. During a high-stress situation like this you do not want to rely on your ability to handle complex motor skills. The officers also were not allowed to train with their duty ammo, which was a .357 Magnum. They had only used .38 special ammunition in training and their unfamiliarity with full power-duty ammunition negatively affected their marksmanship. They were also not familiar with their shotguns, and manipulated the action so fast they ejected a live round. The concept of Contact and Cover was not used when the initial stop was made, and the suspects were easily able to divert the officers' attention to take advantage.

For several years it was believed that one of the officers had spent shell casings in his pockets from when he reloaded. It was reported that officers' learned this "training scar" during weapons training to keep the range clean. It was an example used by many trainers of what you practice in training will occur in real life. It is not known where this myth started, but that is what it is—a myth.

The Newhall Incident significantly changed training standards and practices. By learning from the lessons of went wrong that night (by no fault of the officers involved), we have improved the survival chances of all future generations of police officers.

This is why training and learning from the experiences of others is so important.

Chapter 12   Give Back—Become an Instructor

> *If you know the enemy and know yourself, you need not fear the result of a hundred battles. If you know yourself but not the enemy, for every victory gained you will also suffer a defeat. If you know neither the enemy nor yourself, you will succumb in every battle.*
>
> —Sun Tzu (Giles)

Without someone to help us along the way, we are forced to learn how to do everything by trial and error. This usually leads to learning it the wrong way, or the hardest way, first. Then with some hard-earned experience we come to find there is an easier and smarter way to accomplish what we originally set out to do. (Ever try building something you had never seen before without reading the instructions first? How did that usually work out for you?)

When someone comes along willing to share their experiences we should take notice of what they have to say. If their ideas are viable and make sense, use them. If they are not, you can choose to disregard them. You should also keep those bad ideas in mind so you do not end up repeating the same mistakes again or doing something that you do not think will actually work.

All of our lives we will be faced with new situations in which we will be forced to learn new things and acquire new skills. We will always be, and always should be, in a state of learning. There is just simply no way we can know it all. (Unless you are the average 15-year-old teenager.)

Sun Tzu recognized the importance of constantly learning from others. He analyzed successes and failures in combat and recorded his observations in a book. Therefore, others could benefit from what he had learned. He could easily have kept his lessons to himself, but he chose to train others and share his knowledge to ultimately save lives and, of course, win wars. Sun Tzu understood that by learning new ideas and concepts and then practicing them, we have a better understanding of ourselves and what we are capable of. This shows us our strengths and weaknesses and then guides us on what we need to learn and improve on to do our jobs better.

As law enforcement officers we need to ensure we are as prepared as we can be for the streets. It is also our responsibility to make sure our partners and fellow officers are just has prepared. There is no way you can do this all by yourself. You will certainly have help along the way from many sources, but if you fail to heed that help, it will not only hurt you but possibly your partner or someone else as well.

From the beginning of any career you get help. For those in the military, you certainly got it on Day One when you were introduced to your Drill Sergeant. On that day you may have had a few choice words for him, but I am sure at the end of your training cycle you learned more from him than you had thought possible. The same goes for coaches, teachers, academy instructors and Field Training Officers. These are the people that are passing on all of the institutional knowledge that has accumulated over the years in their particular field. This knowledge is at times learned the hard way in law enforcement, with officers being injured or killed in the process. Such knowledge can also be learned from officers doing something wrong deliberately, either maliciously or criminally. These officers usually find themselves getting suspended, fired or even arrested. This is part of the knowledge that properly assimilated will help you make it to retirement and beyond.

I have always had great respect for the teaching profession, especially after I spent three years as the School Resource Officer at our local high school. The willingness of the teachers and staff to go the extra mile to help their students was evident across the board. I saw that same willingness while growing up in my own teachers, my Army Drill Instructors, Police Academy Instructors and from my Field Training Officers. What a noble thing it is to be willing to step up to the plate to teach and pass on knowledge.

I am a strong believer that we all have an obligation to give back to the career that we have chosen. The best way to do this in law enforcement is to pass on knowledge by teaching and helping instruct your fellow officers. Every one of us excel in a particular subject or topic. Take that interest and drive and pass on what you have learned and experienced as best you can to other officers.

The training does not always have to be in a formal classroom setting. The vast majority of practical and institutional knowledge is passed along while talking with fellow officers after calls or in daily roll call training and discussion.

We can also learn a great deal by conducting formal and informal debriefings after calls with the officers that were involved. An honest assessment must be made about what went right and what went wrong during the incident if we are to learn from it. This level of honesty and bluntness can be a hard thing to do, but it must be done if we are to gain any benefit from the debriefing. For debriefings to be effective, everyone must be willing to give input and understand that feelings maybe hurt, even your own.

If you get the chance to conduct some formal roll call training or departmentwide training take it. You will have a greater impact for your organization in the long run instead of just being a participant at training. You will force yourself to learn more about what you know and do not know about a particular topic. To effectively teach a subject you definitely must be a "subject matter expert" on that topic. However, it will be painfully obvious to everyone if you are not and extremely embarrassing to you. This experience will also give you an opportunity to establish yourself within the department as an expert and the go-to guy when a question related to your area of expertise arises.

A popular area of interest where you see officers wanting to become instructors is with firearms. It's great if you choose this area, but realize it is much more than knowing how to handle a firearm. A true firearms instructor is a use-of-force expert, which means you should also be familiar with defensive tactics and understand all of the liability issues that come with the use of force. Being tactically proficient and current on officer safety topics and trends are also essential. Instructors need to be familiar with all the weapon systems their agency uses, and they should know how to maintain and repair them. Other common instructorships include Defensive Tactics Instructors, EVOC Instructors, Report Writing, Computer Use, Evidence Collection, Narcotics and the list goes on and on.

Once you have decided what you want to teach, you need to become familiar with who you are going to instruct. Teaching a group of senior police officer is completely different than teaching recruits in the Academy. So, if you want to be a good instructor, it is vitally important to take the time to understand your students, because everyone learns in their own way and it might not be the way you teach. Some students are Visual/Verbal learners and prefer to read the material. Others are Tactile learners and need to learn by going hands on. Some students need to see diagrams and charts, whereas others just need to listen to a lecture. If possible, try to incorporate several Learning Styles into your presentations to offer students with the best opportunity to get the most out of the class.

To do this, you need to understand the five different types of Teaching Styles and decide which one, or which combination of the five, works best for you. The styles are called Expert (displays a detailed level of knowledge), Formal (focuses on clear expectations), Personal (believes in teaching by example), Facilitator (emphasizes teacher-student interactions) and Delegator (develops capacity to function autonomously). All of these have Pros and Cons. I would suggest you do some research into these styles and identify your current teaching method and then find ways to incorporate parts of the other styles into your teaching. This approach will ensure you reach the most students.

In regard to student learning styles, on average, out of every 10 students 2 will be Auditory learners, 4 will be Visual and 4 will be Tactile. Without proper instructor training, most learning (close to 90%) is done strictly by lecture so only 2 of the 10 students will benefit from the class. (For a detailed look at Teaching and Learning Principles, I highly recommend you read Chapter 2 of the book *Train to Win* by Wes Doss, 2003.)

Once you are assigned to teach a class or become an Instructor it is important that you continue to improve your personal skill level, which will help develop your confidence level in the teaching of the topic you have chosen.

This confidence also translates to your actions on the street and how you perform your regular duties. It builds your winning mind-set, which is always important to have. You should always be in a state of learning and trying to find ways to stay current and up-to-date.

If you are not proficient in your skills and your enemy has taken the time to train and prepare himself better, Sun Tzu predicts you will lose in battle. Sun Tzu famously stated, *If you know the enemy and know yourself, you need not fear the result of a hundred battles. If you know yourself but not the enemy, for every victory gained you will also suffer a defeat. If you know neither the enemy nor yourself, you will succumb in every battle.*

If you do not study what your enemy is doing and concentrate only on yourself, you have evened the playing field and your chances are now equal. Sun Tzu recognized the value of preparation and training to succeed. When you know yourself and your abilities and have taken the time to study and learn what your opponent is capable of, you have greatly enhanced your chances of survival in your favor. Because of this it is important to share your knowledge with other officers so we can all survive on the streets.

Key Points

- Share your knowledge.

- Become proficient in your area of expertise in order to teach it.

- Understand teaching and learning Styles.

- Always learn from others.

- Know your enemy.

Chapter 13 Improve Your Communication Skills

> *Gongs and drums, banners and flags, are means whereby the ears and eyes of the host may be focused on one particular point.*
> —Sun Tzu

Without an excellent grasp of proper communication skills and techniques we would not be able to succeed at our jobs. Communication among our coworkers, citizens, victims and suspects is an everyday occurrence. That is why we must master our communication skills if we want to be effective. Let us look at some examples of how we can improve those skills.

First of all, what is true communication? Is it simply telling someone what to do and expect them to do it? The answer to that is no. That is an example of one-way communication, which is rarely productive. True communication involves sending a message and then receiving a reply and having both parties involved understand what is going on. Where we as police officers commonly see this definition of communication fail is when we communicate to dispatchers or other officers over the radio. From personal and professional experience I can attest to how dispatchers and officers fail to effectively communicate. Professionally, I have never been a dispatcher because I realize how hard that job can be, but I have worked with them extensively throughout my career and understand their job. Personally, I did end up marrying a dispatcher and, therefore, I can hear from her firsthand the complaints that they have on how we communicate from the streets to dispatch.

Most of the complaints regarding communicating over the radio can simply be solved by doing one thing: slowing down. Think about what you want to say, take a deep breath, key up your mic and then talk. If you speak too fast or cut off half your transmission by not keying up first, you end up wasting a lot of valuable airtime that may be needed by other officers when you are asked to repeat what you initially said. It is also important to be concise in your transmission, so pick your words carefully. Some agencies use specific radio or "10-codes" to shorten their transmissions and to clarify the message they are trying to send. This system most often works well but, in times of stress, you may have to rely on plain language to get your point across. This is because there is a danger of having multiple interpretations of a code, which can lead to misunderstandings. Therefore, when in doubt, plain English is always best. Sun Tzu warns us when he discusses communication *that when it fails, a whole army may be robbed of its spirits. A command and control may be robbed of his presence of mind.*

Here is an example of how communication on the radio can go wrong when words sound alike and you are in a stressful situation. My department's SWAT Team was formed in 1997, and on one of our first activations we were attempting to arrest a suspect that was wanted for assaulting one of our officers. The suspect was located at a local hotel with his girlfriend. We surrounded the area and evacuated nearby rooms before placing a call to him. I was on the outer perimeter with other officers securing his escape route. When we made contact with him via telephone he initially complied and walked out of the room. When he saw the SWAT Team and realized he was going to jail, he suddenly changed his mind and rushed back into his room. Over the radio we heard a very excited officer yell, "He's got a gun!", which was followed by two muffled shotgun blasts. Talk about pucker factor. Here we are on one of our first activations and we are involved in a shooting. However, what was actually transmitted was "He's gonna run" and then two less-lethal beanbag rounds were fired at him. This simple misunderstanding could have greatly changed the outcome of the situation if he had suddenly emerged from the rear hotel room window attempting to escape. Everything was eventually clarified and after 30 minutes with his girlfriend, a little negotiating and a sore leg from the bean bag round, he surrendered to us without further incident.

Another common example of miscommunication you need to be aware of, especially in the tactical environment, is the use of the word "Go" to initiate an action. Unfortunately, it sure sounds like "No." Think about the dangers here. You are first in the stack waiting at the door and someone starts yelling "No, No, No" to stop you from going because they have spotted a potential threat.

All you hear is "Go, Go, Go" and you take off. This could lead to a lot of hurt if the threat was some sort of booby trap or an armed suspect aiming at the door. Therefore, we stopped using the word "Go" to initiate team movement. We now use the word "Execute." There are not many words that rhyme with "execute" that can cause problems. We save the word "No" for what it really means—danger areas.

Your communication skills are especially important when dealing with suspects. How you talk with them and how they perceive you can determine whether you will need to resort to force to take someone into custody or if they will simply comply. Remember, after your presence, your verbal skills are the next and most common level of force. Officers that end up in a lot of fights, engage in use of force incidents and have a high number of citizen complaints usually do not communicate well and rely on intimidation and brute force to get their point across. These officers may not have a great deal of self-esteem and are not usually confident with their abilities to speak with people to get them to comply. Granted, talking with people is a skill that takes some time and a lot of practice to master, but it is something we all need to develop and work on. I always enjoyed it when someone would tell me "Thank you" after I issued them a citation. I considered that a win.

Do not forget the other end of the communication spectrum in which you are dealing with the victims. Your level of compassion and understanding really needs to come into play here, especially when conducting domestic violence and sexual assault investigations. You may have to ask some very personal and intimate questions that are embarrassing to the victim but necessary for the investigation. It can be difficult for officers to turn off the tough street cop exterior and turn on the compassionate officer persona. This takes practice and does not come naturally to many people. If you have the chance to take supplemental training in this area, be sure you do not pass up the opportunity. It will turn out to be a great benefit to you.

An even more specialized communication skill comes into play when dealing with juvenile victims. There are a whole new set of rules and techniques you need to master to obtain a useful statement. While I was a detective I was assigned to our Juvenile Unit and obtained some specialized training in interviewing young child abuse victims, but it was still not nearly enough to truly feel competent in this area. I was always impressed with the trained Child Forensic Interviewers and the rapport they built with very young crime victims and the information they obtained. It is definitely an acquired skill that we should all have some familiarity with if we want to be successful when we find ourselves interviewing children.

Sun Tzu realized that communication is an integral and important part of warfare. The spoken word does not travel far, especially in battle, so a system of banners and flags had to be developed to relay messages. In Sun Tzu's time they also used drums and gongs at night to communicate because the banners and flags could not be seen. This system continued throughout history until the telegraph, telephones and radios were invented. Even in today's high-tech world we still see the use of banners and flags when everything else fails.

In military and law enforcement, commands and the order in which they are given have to be concise and direct, so that every-one understands what needs to get done, especially in an emer-gency. This principle also applies in our everyday communication skills. We need to master these skills to succeed in this profession, so, when time is of the essence, you will be able to deliver effective directions to both officers and civilians, which is a far different form of communication than simply asking for cooperation in a casual and friendly manner. Although this may work, doing so opens the possibility of the recipient questioning what you want done and trying to come up with an alternative. When there is no time to waste, you must develop your command presence so when you issue a command it is followed.

Do not forget the important lesson of good communication skills mentioned in the Introduction of this book that Sun Tzu gave to the Emperor of Wu when he was asked to provide a demonstration of his skills in training the troops. Sun Tzu gathered the Emperor's concubines and gave them commands that were ignored. He explained that if the commands were not followed because the orders were not clear and concise, it was the fault of the general. If, however, the commands were clear and concise and the commands were not followed, it was the fault of the officers. I am sure the first two concubines that were chosen to lead wished they had had a better understanding of good communication skills. Remember their fates.

Key Points

- Practice your communication skills.

- Slow down.

- Be clear and avoid similar sounding phrases.

- Obtain specialized training if available.

- Be able to issue clear and concise commands.

Chapter 14   Win with Verbal Judo

> *Hence to fight and conquer in all your battles is not supreme excellence; supreme excellence consists in breaking the enemy's resistance without fighting.*
>
> —Sun Tzu (Giles)

The ultimate goal of all police officers should be to go home at the end of your shift safely and then to retire healthy and uninjured. Fortunately, owing to better training and equipment, the odds of this happening continue to improve. However, we must not forget it is still a dangerous world out there. We cannot predict when we will be called upon to go into harm's way and "do battle" with the bad guys. When we do go, it would be great if just by our mere presence everyone on scene would simply comply upon our arrival, and when we leave everyone is smiling and saying what a wonderful job we did.

We know, however, that is not going to happen on every call for service, so let us look at reality. Say you are dispatched to a disturbance call and when you get there you find two subjects in a heated argument. You try to intervene to calm the situation but are met with "F*%k you cop. We'll take care of this ourselves." I am sure they will, but they probably won't do it legally. Your job is to make sure no one gets hurt and the argument does not escalate into something physical.

Because we are dealing with a disturbance that is currently only verbal, we cannot always come in with our guns drawn yelling for everyone to get on the ground (however, in some circumstances that is exactly what we have to do). Because we do not yet know all of the reasons why they are arguing, we still must be cognizant of any and all dangers that might arise and be prepared to react to them. So what do we have at our disposal that can be used to de-escalate this situation?

Most Use of Force Continuum Charts define various levels of force options and at what levels those options can be called upon. The first level of force usually mentioned is "Officer's Presence."

This is how you present yourself just by showing up. Do you look professional and in charge, or do you look like an uncaring slob. Just your command presence usually works on the good people out there that respect law enforcement, and when they see the uniform and badge they comply. Let's say in this situation our mere presence did not work, and we need to try something else. The second option is the use of Verbal Commands, which should be attempted before any hands on or control holds are used. (Unless the situation demands an immediate physical or deadly force option be used.)

Sun Tzu recognized that if a soldier can win his battles without fighting and prevents the loss of life (either yours or the enemies) that this should be the outcome we strive for. He wrote, ***In the practical art of war, the best thing of all is to take the enemy's country whole and intact. Supreme excellence consists in breaking the enemy's resistance without fighting.*** This is also what you should be striving for when handling all of your calls for service. If you can get the suspect to comply and/or surrender peacefully without using force then you are doing a greater service to your community in the long run and improving your odds of not having to injure the suspect, or of getting injured yourself.

A former police officer and English professor, the late George Thompson, coined the phrase "verbal judo" back in the early 1990s after he recognized that law enforcement officers were engaged in a form of fighting, usually with words only, when they interacted with subjects on the street. Every time we make contact with someone we normally have the need to talk with them. From completing a Field Identification Card, to issuing a citation, to making an arrest, we all use words to convey what we want the suspect to do. How we speak and interact with people has changed over the years and thanks to the techniques taught in Verbal Judo our compliance rate has increased and the number of complaints against the police have dropped.

So what is Verbal Judo and how can we use it to win our battles (or at least most of them) when dealing with people? The way it was first explained to me many years ago is that it is a way to get people to comply with you without them realizing you are influencing their decision to do so. By using the subject's own words against him, and providing only the options that you want, you can gain your desired outcome the majority of the time. However, there will always be those few out there that, no matter what you say or do, will make it necessary to use other options to accomplish your goals.

The concepts of Verbal Judo are simple in principle, but may be hard to employ because we let our egos get in the way. We often fall into the verbal traps of suspects and, when we respond, we give their arguments credibility. What we need to do is to learn to defuse the situation by redirecting them, answering their questions and explaining what is going on. A major part of this process is showing empathy for what the person is going through. Try to see the situation from their point of view and then explain what you are able to do. By always remaining professional you will defuse most situations. You have to be in control of yourself in order to create control.

In general, there are five steps to a successful contact with citizens: (1) Listen to what they have to say. (2) Empathize with their situation. (3) Ask questions to find out more about the situation. (4) Paraphrase what has been said. (5) Summarize the entire contact. Following this format will usually work out in your favor.

In George Thompson's book, *Verbal Judo*, there is a list of 11 things that you should never say to someone. I suggest you read the entire book so that you have an in-depth understanding of what they are before overlooking one to your detriment. An example of one thing you should not say to someone is "What is your problem?" This immediately puts that person on the defensive. If the citizen is irate and yelling and you start yelling back at them to "Calm down," all you will do is make them even angrier. Before you start yelling, try using the five steps and I think you will be impressed.

Remember that Sun Tzu's principle of winning without fighting should always be your goal. However, if that does not happen, it doesn't hurt to carry a big stick behind you when attempting to utilize the principles of Verbal Judo.

It is also important to never let your guard down when dealing with suspects. You should always be prepared for the possibility that Verbal Judo is being used against you. (Have you ever been talked out of giving a ticket?) Streetwise criminals know what they are doing and will take every opportunity to "become your friend" to gain an advantage. This advantage could lead to an escape attempt or an assault.

You may think you have the gift of gab and can talk to everyone, but if that fails you must also be prepared to react with physical force if the situation calls for it. Verbal Judo should be just one of many parts of your personal officer-safety repertoire.

A good understanding of the principles used in Verbal Judo will greatly enhance your safety. It will also assist you in fulfilling one of Sun Tzu's tenants, which states, ***supreme excellence consists in breaking the enemy's resistance without fighting.***

Key Points

- Winning the conflict without fighting is your goal.

- Understand how to control subjects with your words only.

- Be prepared to escalate.

- Do not become a victim of verbal judo.

Chapter 15　Community Policing—
An Overall Approach

> *To win battles and capture lands and cities, but to fail to consolidate these achievements is ominous and may be described as a waste of time and resources.*
>
> —Sun Tzu

Many officers do not realize the importance of "community policing" and the countless benefits that come with implementing such a philosophy. These benefits include greater communication between the public and law enforcement, which can lead to a reduction in crime. It may not seem like a part of an "officer safety plan," but it should. Community policing can markedly enhance your overall safety program by eliminating all, or most, of the threats we face. If we can subdue our enemy without fighting, we win, which is a core concept in community policing. We need to anticipate where our future problems will arise and decide how we can combat those problems before they actually happen. Sun Tzu recognized this concept when he wrote, *A victorious army seeks its victories before seeking battle. An army destined to defeat fights in the hopes of winning.*

What exactly is Community Policing? In short, it is a policing philosophy that incorporates community partnerships and organizational changes within a department to solve the problems affecting a community. This proposal evolved in the 1980s with the Broken Window Theory, which asserted that when small problems are ignored by traditional policing, bigger problems will ensue. However, by tackling smaller problems by working with the community, bigger problems can be avoided. By changing the culture of our law enforcement community and working closely with the citizens in our jurisdictions, we can eliminate some of the problems we are likely to encounter before we have to resort to more reactive and forceful tactics.

In reality, Community Policing should not be a specific program within the department but should be a departmentwide philosophy. Some officers may be resistive to community policing because they feel that their primary job is to arrest the bad guys and take them to jail. Yes, that is and always will be an important part of the job, but it's not the only part. If we can prevent the bad guy from even being there in the first place, it would make our jobs all that much easier. It is vital that we take the time to enlist the help of the citizens in our community so we can make the area safer for all.

The community policing philosophy is not a thing to be avoided. In fact, it should be embraced by the entire department. Some officers may not be willing, or just feel uncomfortable, in going to neighborhood gatherings, visiting schools or attending community meetings, but someone needs to do these things. The officers not willing to participate had better be willing to take a few extra calls and reports and then cover the beats of the officers who are attending these events. Everyone in your department wears the same patch on their sleeves, so you should all share a sense of teamwork and be willing to work toward the same goals.

I spent two years specifically assigned to a community policing unit in the late 1990s when the concept was still being introduced in police work. At this point the philosophy was not departmentwide and only used within the specific unit. There was definitely an us versus them mentality in my department at the time. Regular patrol officers thought we were wimping out and becoming soft, and we kept thinking "they just don't get it," because we were actually making a bigger difference.

Community Policing did take some getting used to, especially having to attend community meetings and listening to citizens' complaints. It was even harder at these meetings to not speak our minds and say the things we subconsciously wanted to. Some of the complaints were legitimate criminal problems that needed to be dealt with. Whereas others we would just sit back and say to ourselves, "What the heck is he talking about?" Although these issues may not have been criminal in nature, they were important to those citizens. We worked hard to solve as many of these problems as we could, because we certainly could not have solved them all. We were definitely a good resource and a conduit to coordinate help from the proper agency or department within the city to the citizens within our community that needed it.

I included this chapter because I think it is important to look at Sun Tzu's philosophy and see how it applies. If we arrest only the current bad guys, we solve only that initial and lone problem. We are not solving any of the long-term issues that brought about those bad guys in the first place. Our ultimate utopian goal would be to establish a community where law enforcement is not even needed. Although we all know that will never happen, it should be the goal we are working toward. It would be nice to live in a society where our law enforcement presence is not needed as much as it is now. One way to remedy this is working toward long-term solutions to solving problems, which can be done in large part by implementing a community policing philosophy.

Without that mind-set, all of our hard work in arresting our current crop of bad guys will do nothing toward preventing the next generation of bad guys from showing up in your neighborhood. We need to focus on the social issues that encourage and enable our young people to commit crimes in the first place. We need to spend a large amount of time with the youth of our community to ensure they stay on the right path. The best way to do this is to establish a collaborative working relationship with other organizations that can help in ways law enforcement cannot do alone. Programs that have worked in the past include establishing Neighborhood Watch Programs, Citizen's Police Academies, Homeless Outreach Programs, Police Bicycle Patrols and connecting with the community directly using social media. We can no longer work by ourselves to solve problems. We simply do not have all the resources or the budget. If we do not make the effort now, both individually and as an organization, we are sure to lose ground in the future and, as Sun Tzu predicted, it would be ***ominous and may be described as a waste of time and resources.***

Key Points

- Establish and support a departmentwide community policing philosophy.

- Realize it is also an officer safety issue.

- Work collaboratively with other agencies to improve officer safety.

- Focus on our youth.

Chapter 16   Establish Your Leadership Skills

> *If in training soldiers, commands are habitually enforced, the army will be well disciplined; if not, it's discipline will be bad. If a general shows confidence in his men but always insists on his orders being obeyed, the gain will be mutual.*
>
> —Sun Tzu

All of us have leadership traits somewhere within us. Some individuals show these traits better than others. Then there are those that seem to be natural leaders. We all have met or know of someone like this. They are the ones we will naturally follow and trust, whether they are wearing rank or not. It is hoped that you have some of these individuals in your department. Maybe you are that guy? Or gal? These are the go-to officers when the situation is turning bad and someone needs to step up and take charge. Sometimes these are also the ones the Sergeants and other supervisors may even turn to for advice.

Of course, there are some out there that consider themselves leaders simply because they were promoted by either scoring really high on a test, or by being drinking buddies with the Chief. In fact, these "leaders" usually turn out to be merely managers of personnel. You better realize early on that there is a big difference between being a leader and being a manager. We should all be well aware of who is who.

The true leaders are the ones that step up and make a difference. They are the ones that lead from the front and figure out the better way to get something done. Leaders are the ones that make changes for the better. Managers, on the other hand, simply enforce policy and are afraid of change. They do not think outside the box. Managers are there simply to make sure everything remains status quo. It has been said that managers simply manage and apply the rules, whereas leaders lead and make the rules. It is usually pretty apparent what type of individual you are dealing with. It is also important to remember that true leaders also know how to manage, but the managers rarely know how to lead. In a chaotic situation where things are happening way outside of the box you do not want the manager in charge who has only been trained to operate within the box.

Leadership is a great responsibility that some of us actively seek out for the challenge and are willing to be the one people look up to for guidance. A leadership role can also be thrust upon you even if you have never been actively looking for it. How many times in combat has a private or corporal been forced to step up and take charge when their leader is no longer available? It is important to remember that in police work the first officer on scene, even if he is a rookie is in charge until relieved by a supervisor or a senior officer.

There are also those who seek out leadership roles for the wrong reason. These people just want to be in charge, tell people what to do, check off the "shows leadership" box on an evaluation and to build their own egos by wearing the stripes or bars. These so-called leaders rarely garner the respect of their troops and are usually looked upon as a liability.

One essential aspect of leadership that some may find difficult is to issue orders that may not be popular but are vital for the operation. If you are in-charge, your troops must be willing to follow you and trust your judgment that the orders are important and justified. If they cannot to do that and have no confidence in you, discipline will be bad and the mission will fail. If the troops confidence level is high and you are a trusted leader, they will follow your orders, which will increase your chances of mission success. It is up to you to instill that confidence, especially when your troops are not receptive to the plan or the policy in the first place. The best way for you to do that is to lead by example. If you are willing to follow the policy or the plan of your superiors, the troops should be also. However, if you are not willing to do so for whatever reason, why should they? Sun Tzu recognized that confidence in your superiors and in your subordinates is a two-way street when he wrote, *If a general shows confidence in his men but always insists on his orders being obeyed, the gain will be mutual.*

In most professions, and especially in police work, the first-line supervisor is one of the most challenging and rewarding positions you can have within your department. Everything revolves around you. You are the middle management that needs to work with the Chief and Command Staff implementing their policies. You also need to work with the line officers to ensure their well-being and bring their concerns forward to the Chief. In this position you will definitely not be able to make everyone happy, but you are certainly expected to.

When you become a supervisor or a team leader, you will have a great number of demands placed upon you. You will be required to make on-the-spot decisions that can have long-term consequences. You will need to keep your people motivated so they continue to do a good job and represent the department in a positive light. You will need to be the disciplinarian that enforces the department's policies and ensure everyone is following the rules and doing the right thing. You are also the trainer and expected to teach your newer officers what it takes to become a successful police officer. You will also need to be the counselor and shoulder to cry on when someone on your team experiences a critical event and is having a difficult time dealing with it.

These are just some of the aspects of leadership that you have to be prepared for. According to Sun Tzu, successful leaders should *regard your soldiers as your children, and they will follow you into the deepest valleys; look upon them as your own beloved sons, and they will stand by you even unto death.* He understood the importance of looking out for subordinates.

These responsibilities are not just for patrol supervisors and office managers but are also for the team leaders of specialized units. For example, a SWAT Team Leader is going in the door with his officers and is right there with them making the quick and important decisions. In this environment there can be no room for unnecessary hesitation or indecision. These Team Leaders have to take all of the responsibilities of leadership much more seriously because of the immediate life-threatening stakes that are involved. Most SWAT Team Leaders do not get their position without the support of their teammates. Team Leaders have to earn the respect of the team and demonstrate to them their competence in leading. If they cannot do that their team will be dysfunctional and ineffective. Unfortunately, some team leaders are chosen only because they are a supervisor in another unit and the team is in need of a leader. In this case, a patrol sergeant is usually selected and sent off to SWAT school. He or she is then expected to take charge on their return. There is a great learning curve here and most experienced supervisors with the desire to be tactically proficient should be able to perform the job. These individuals are your natural leaders that the troops more than likely already look up to. The supervisors that cannot grasp the tactical aspects of the assignment will not become the leader you need. Additionally, be very cautious of the appointment or selection of a team leader when someone is owed a favor from the Chief or is simply assigned because he has the rank but not the desire.

Officers who are not directly involved in supervising others still must display some leadership skills in police work. What happens at a busy intersection when you are called upon to direct traffic and no one obeys your commands? How do you control the crime scene when the family shows up and starts to interfere? If you are first on scene at any incident, you are in charge until relieved by a higher authority. You will have to utilize your command presence and demonstrate some sort of leadership in all of these situations.

We all have leadership skills and we should be prepared to use them. However, just like any other skill you learn, it takes practice to be successful. We all have it in us so don't be afraid to try. Be aware that you will make mistakes so learn from them and improve.

Sun Tzu recognized the importance of leadership and the importance it plays in successful military operations when he wrote, ***Thus it may be known that the leader of armies is the arbiter of the people's fate, the man on whom it depends whether the nation shall be in peace or in peril.*** This is an important concept and brings to light how important leadership is to everything we do in our chosen profession.

Key Points
<ul><li>Be prepared for the responsibility of leadership.</li><li>Know the difference between managers and leaders.</li><li>Practice your skills.</li></ul>

Chapter 17   Integrity—It's Essential

> *The consummate leader cultivates the moral law, and strictly adheres to method and discipline; thus it is in his power to control success.*
>
> —Sun Tzu (Giles)

If I had to give a one word answer to the question, "What characteristic would be most important for a police officer to have?" My answer would certainly be *integrity*. Without it we simply could not do our jobs effectively. Why is that? What is so important about integrity?

A basic definition of integrity according to *The New Oxford American Dictionary* states "the quality of being honest and having strong moral principals related to moral and ethical decisions based on personal choice," which is basically saying, "doing the right thing all of the time." In fact, Integrity is so important that it is a central theme on the Law Enforcement Code of Ethics, which was adopted in 1957 to be an ethical standard for all law enforcement officers.

As police officers we have been entrusted by the citizens we protect to live by a higher standard and do the right thing, even when no one is looking. This means on and off duty. For example, imagine how you would feel if you were away on vacation and the police responded to your home on an alarm call. The officer finds an unsecured door and while checking out the interior of your residence, decides he wants to take something. When you arrive home, you discover the theft and file a report with the suspect listed as unknown. It is later determined that the officer who had responded to the alarm call was in fact responsible for the theft. He took advantage of his position and the situation and violated the trust we have all placed in him, his department and the profession.

Another example would be if an officer is caught in an outright lie. Perhaps he falsified a report to justify an arrest, or lied on the stand while testifying. Would that officer ever be able to reliably present a case or testify again in court for the remainder of his career? The simple answer to that is "No."

Integrity is such an important aspect of our profession that it often appears in slogans written on the side of patrol cars and in department mission statements. For example, in my department, our mission statement simply reads, "Providing Excellent Service with Integrity and Respect."

I believe Sun Tzu also recognized the importance of Integrity when he referred to the "moral influence." His soldiers and our officers must truly believe they are doing the right thing at all times while performing their official duties. If all involved are working with the same level of integrity (or moral influence), they will avoid conflicts and do what is right at all times. This will endear the troops to their leader, which in turn greatly enhances the chances for success in any endeavor. Sun Tzu wrote, *The Moral Law causes the people to be in complete accord with their ruler.*

We should also be aware of our actions when we are off-duty because seemingly innocent or minor activities such as driving over the speed limit, social drinking with friends and how you relate to others can reflect on your job. Even if the activity is legal, but questionable, officers still need to be careful. Any police officer cited or arrested for something that occurs when they are off-duty and not job related will always garner more media attention than almost any other profession doing the same thing. It is always newsworthy when a cop screws up.

A recent trend that underscores this point is the prevalence of social networking sites and online chat rooms. These sites are fine when used appropriately. Unfortunately, some officers make the mistake of talking about sensitive or confidential activities that occur at work on these sites. Other officers will speak negatively about coworkers, supervisors and their department as a whole. Officers forget these comments can be seen by the general public, which includes city council members and other important public figures. And do not forget about the press. In some cases, even though no disrespect was intended, photos get posted that turn out to be highly inappropriate. I have known officers who have posted pictures of themselves at a crash site and in the background, you can see the victim still under the coroner's blanket. Other officers forget they are in uniform sometimes and pose with a group of citizens in such a way that is inappropriate or that might express their own political views. Not the brightest thing to be doing while on-duty. It has become such an issue that most, if not every departments' General Orders or Policy Manuals will now have a specific section devoted to the use of Social Media.

I can go on and on about various examples of things that are wrong to do, but it should be obvious to all involved that we need to hold ourselves to a higher standard. We have been given great responsibility, authority and power and we should not abuse it in any way. This will only bring discredit upon ourselves, our departments and our profession. Sun Tzu did not have a social media account but he understood how we control our own destinies when he wrote, *To secure ourselves against defeat lies in our own hands.*

So, whose responsibility is it to make sure these lapses of judgment do not happen? Is it your supervisor, your peers, the Chief or Sheriff? To some degree it is all of these, but the most important person that determines your integrity level is you. Remember that you are the one who needs to do the right thing when no one is looking. We should all be striving to "enhance the moral influence" of not just ourselves but all the people we work with. It is our responsibility to step in when we see others straying from what is right. It is not always easy to do this and at times your decision to act will also test your own level of integrity. By doing this, we are ensuring our Departments are operating at the highest standard that we expect of ourselves and that the citizens expect of us.

An Academy Instructor I work with always reminds the recruits that "Every day is an Interview." What a good thing to remind yourself of on a regular basis. You just never know who is watching and you certainly want "that job."

It is important to remember that only by maintaining a high level of integrity on a constant basis can we succeed in our mission of "providing excellent service with integrity and respect."

Key Points

- Without Integrity you have nothing.

- It is everyone's responsibility.

- Watch your conduct on and off duty.

Law Enforcement Code of Ethics

As a law enforcement officer, my fundamental duty is to serve the community; to safeguard lives and property; to protect the innocent against deception, the weak against oppression or intimidation and the peaceful against violence or disorder; and to respect the constitutional rights of all to liberty, equality and justice.

I will keep my private life unsullied as an example to all and will behave in a manner that does not bring discredit to me or to my agency. I will maintain courageous calm in the face of danger, scorn or ridicule; develop self-restraint; and be constantly mindful of the welfare of others. Honest in thought and deed both in my personal and official life, I will be exemplary in obeying the law and the regulations of my department. Whatever I see or hear of a confidential nature or that is confided to me in my official capacity will be kept ever secret unless revelation is necessary in the performance of my duty.

I will never act officiously or permit personal feelings, prejudices, political beliefs, aspirations, animosities or friendships to influence my decisions. With no compromise for crime and with relentless prosecution of criminals, I will enforce the law courteously and appropriately without fear or favor, malice or ill will, never employing unnecessary force or violence and never accepting gratuities.

I recognize the badge of my office as a symbol of public faith, and I accept it as a public trust to be held so long as I am true to the ethics of police service. I will never engage in acts of corruption or bribery, nor will I condone such acts by other police officers. I will cooperate with all legally authorized agencies and their representatives in the pursuit of justice.

I know that I alone am responsible for my own standard of professional performance and will take every reasonable opportunity to enhance and improve my level of knowledge and competence.

I will constantly strive to achieve these objectives and ideals, dedicating myself before God to my chosen profession ... law enforcement.

The International Association of Chiefs of Police adopted the Law Enforcement Code of Ethics at the 64th Annual IACP Conference and Exposition in October 1957. The Code of Ethics stands as a preface to the mission and commitment law enforcement agencies make to the public they serve.

Chapter 18   Plan for Success—Develop an Operation Plan

> *Now the general who wins a battle makes many calculations in his temple before the battle is fought. The general who loses a battle makes but few calculations.*
>
> —Sun Tzu (Giles)

Sun Tzu recognized the importance of preoperational planning when he discussed the need for commanders and generals to plan ahead of their anticipated actions. It should be obvious to everyone how important it is to preplan what you are going to do before you set out to do it. It is also vitally important to rehearse and conduct your training before the big event. We all need to understand that without the proper planning and training we will find ourselves on a path to failure. Sun Tzu said, ***The enlightened ruler lays his plans well ahead; the good general cultivates his resources.***

In our personal lives we plan for almost everything we do, from day-to-day things like taking the kids to school, then to sports practice, to long-term events like entire family vacations and eventually to our retirements. These events may not be overly hard to plan for, but if we don't do them correctly it could turn out to be disastrous.

In law enforcement we are continually planning for special events, including preparation for natural disasters, large public gatherings, training exercises, special operations and SWAT callouts to name but just a few. These events usually take a higher level of attention and planning because of their complex nature.

In law enforcement there are several different systems designed to assist with planning that have made the process that much easier. These systems come in different forms but are usually referred to as "operations plans" or "Op Plans." The American military has mastered their system, because you can imagine the logistical nightmare it would be to conduct small-

and large-scale military operations without a formal plan. These plans on a reduced scale are also useful for the team leader of a small unit. Minus a specified way to organize our needs we are sure to miss something during the planning phase that will likely be needed during the operation. It could be something as simple as making sure everyone is on the right radio channel.

In law enforcement it is a common practice for SWAT Teams and other specialized units to write up an Operations Plan to ensure they have covered most, if not all, contingencies associated with the operation they are about to go on. This Op Plan is then distributed and briefed to all involved so everyone is familiar with their individual role and the goal of the operation. It is important that everyone understands how the mission is to be carried out. These plans should be simple and easy to understand so there is no confusion about your responsibilities and the rest of the team's. The Operation Plan format can also be used for almost any event that requires some sort of formalized planning. You may need to add or delete certain segments depending on the event, but essentially they are all the same.

Being thorough is the key to success when planning operations and special events. Sun Tzu understood this when he stated, *It is by attention to this point that I can foresee who is likely to win or lose.* You will want to try and cover all the possible contingencies. However, you should not go into too many fine details about how each operator should carry out his assignment. If you try to document everyone's actions down to the smallest minute detail, your operation orders will be overly long and confusing, which will most probably lead to mistakes that could cost you the entire operation. Your operation plan should cover the mission and what needs to get done. Your training should cover the rest.

There is an old saying that "all plans are great until the first bullet comes your way, then all your plans are out the window." This is why training and proper preparation are so important. One way to deal with the potential for chaos in any operation is to plan for possible mishaps such as shots fired, officer down, a disabled vehicle, bad communications or breaching problems. These are the types of things that could happen on any mission. Room for adaptability should always be considered when planning your operations. Unknown circumstances are always sure to arise just prior to or during your operation and you should be prepared to respond to them if you want to succeed. Be careful not to get bogged down with everything that could possibly happen, and focus on what will probably happen.

When looking for examples of Operation Plans, the largest and I would say one of the most complex and important would be the plan for Operation Overlord, which has simply come to be known as D-Day.

In World War II the allies understood that to win the European Campaign they would have to invade the European mainland. They began planning for that operation in early 1942 and after several years of planning and training the operation commenced on June 6, 1944 (D-Day). The planners realized the fight to get off the beach and through the Atlantic Wall would be a hard one. They also had to allow for the fact that by 1944 American soldiers had been at war for three years and may be reluctant to commit to a fight that some thought would be unsuccessful. To overcome this particular obstacle in the plan, a majority of the troops assigned to the D-Day invasion had never been in actual combat. The thinking was that if they did not know what to expect about the horror of battle they would be more willing to go. In this instance, the planners were utilizing one of Sun Tzu's principles whether they realized it or not. Sun Tzu said, *Soldiers when in desperate straits lose the sense of fear. If there is no place of refuge, they will stand firm. If they are in hostile country, they will show a stubborn front. If there is no help for it, they will fight hard.* The beaches of Normandy provided all of these conditions and American soldiers, along with their allies, prevailed. They fought their way off the beaches and set the tone for the remainder of the war. The planning did not stop there. It continued for another year until the war was won.

The success of D-Day could not have occurred without the planners who organized the operation and provided all of the logistical and training support. The invasion force consisted of over 6,900 ships and landing craft, 9,500 aircraft and 155,000 soldiers from three different nations sent to land on the beaches in a single day. Of course, the soldiers and sailors who actually fought the battle deserve a great deal of credit, if not most for the success of D-Day. But for the planners, the trainers and all of the support personnel, the soldiers would never have gotten to the beach or been able to parachute inland in the first place.

Now, not all of us will find ourselves storming enemy-held beaches or planning the invasion of a hostile nation, but we may find ourselves as part of an entry team standing outside a door preparing to make entry on a subject or subjects that could possibly be armed. It is hoped that you have planned and trained for the operation before the order to execute is given. Once you start to move, you will need to be prepared for all sorts of potential contingencies, ranging from having no one home at the target house to having your partner or yourself get shot deep inside of the structure. Planning ahead of time for such contingencies is extremely important for a successful response to events such as an Active Shooter Incident, which would not be the time to start thinking about how you want to respond.

This is a circumstance where a good Operations Order or Plan comes in handy. With the plan detailed in writing, everyone knows what they are supposed to do and how to anticipate unexpected contingencies ahead of time. Although Special Operation Plan formats will vary from agency to agency, universally they all contain essentially the same information. Some of the topics to include in your plan are an overview of the operation, your communication resources, command and allied agency notifications, medical support, suspect and location information, any known hazards, team member assignments and contingency plan responses.

On a different level, firefighters have used a system called the Incident Command System (ICS) since the 1970s in which they have categorized the basic components of their operations. Their op plans are boxed out to identify each category and who is responsible for what. These plans are useful when conducting operations during local disasters or for any large-scale event. The main components of the ICS system are Command, Operations, Planning, Logistics and Finance. This system was modified by the federal government and in 2004 the Department of Homeland Security instituted what is now called NIMS (National Incident Management System).

The ICS system can be used for almost every event that law enforcement encounters, from major criminal investigations to large public events. One of the requirements for ICS is to do prior planning so when an actual event occurs, you can simply plug in the information that corresponds to that particular incident, which saves time and resources. The system itself looks formidable, but once you understand the concept it is fairly easy to implement (hey, the fireman can do it so it must be).

When planning tactical operations, Sgt. Papenfuhs of the San Jose Police Department in California wrote an article about a system he calls "The 6 S's." This system provides for the best possibility of success. The elements of the system to take into account are (1) Superior Numbers, (2) Superior Tools, (3) Superior Tactics, (4) Speed, (5) Surprise and (6) Simple Plan. If you can plan for and incorporate these principles into your operation plan, especially #6, you are on your way to a successful operation. All of these concepts are related to Sun Tzu's principles in one way or another.

To write up a workable operation plan, you need to gather information and intelligence about your objective. Sun Tzu recognized five areas in which a commander should be familiar with when planning. He wrote, ***The art of war is governed by five constant factors, to be taken into account in one's deliberations, when seeking to determine the conditions obtained in the field.*** The "five constant factors" Sun Tzu refers to are The Moral Influence (Integrity), Heaven (environment), Earth (the terrain), the Commander (leadership) and Method (the 5 W's). Sun Tzu continues, ***These five heads should be familiar to every general; he who knows them will be victorious; he who knows them not will fail.***

Another important aspect in planning for law enforcement operations, especially in tactical situations, is to scheme from your adversary's point of view. What is his goal? What is his strategy to accomplish his goal? Where are his escape routes? What resources does he have at his disposal? Put yourself in his shoes and plan his operation for him. Once you have deduced his plan, start counteracting it. By going through this process you might discover things in your own plan that you could have overlooked without studying the incident from your opponent's point of view.

Part of preparing effective Operation Plans should include doing research ahead of time on potential targets in your area. Such preparation will save time, when time is often mission critical. If you have the responsibility of planning a protection detail or need to do a threat assessment for facilities in your jurisdiction, using the following technique can be very helpful. The military uses a system called the CARVER Vulnerability Assessment, which allows you to assess the potential threats to a particular location. CARVER stands for Criticality, Accessibility, Recoverability, Vulnerability, Effect and Recognizability. Using this system, you can develop Target Folders for important facilities that may become targets for terrorists or simply for local criminal activity. When you do your target folders, start with the more high-profile locations and work your way down. Remember that any business or facility can be a target so you will have to prioritize your efforts depending on your own criteria. Sun Tzu also realized how important obtaining knowledge of locations, supply routes and enemy dispositions were when he wrote, *Thus, what enables the wise sovereign and the good general to strike and conquer, and achieve things beyond the reach of ordinary men, is foreknowledge.* The target folders that you prepare ahead of time provides you with the majority of this foreknowledge, which greatly enhances your chances of success.

When preparing your Target Folders you may develop information that a particular location has a greater chance of being attacked, or compromised in some way; therefore, plan some training there for your patrol officers and SWAT Team. School Resource Officers are an excellent resource to engage for training at your local schools. Schools are usually pretty high up on the priority list in most jurisdictions as locations for possible attacks. Schools are the one location that all patrol officers should have a good understanding of and a worthy location of a detailed Target Folder. Having firsthand knowledge of any location is invaluable. If conducting training at the location is not practical, at the minimum you should do a walk through to familiarize yourself with the nuances associated with that location and then encourage everyone else to do the same.

Whenever possible, take the time to plan out your operations thoroughly and do all your research ahead of time. Accounting for all the possible contingencies will save you time and heartache if something should go wrong. When an emergency occurs or if the incident is time sensitive, you will realize that this is not the best time to start your planning. The time you save by preplanning can saves lives.

It is also important to remember that sometimes you may not have a lot of time to come up with a complete Operations Order; therefore, having the basic understanding of what you need to cover in a short amount of planning time is vitally important. A quick plan on a whiteboard is always better than nothing. Once the plan is agreed upon and set in motion stick with it. General Patton would often tell his subordinates when they began planning operations, "A good plan, violently executed now, is better than a perfect plan next week."

Remember the importance of what Sun Tzu said, ***Enlightened rulers must deliberate on the plans to go to war.*** Preplanning is your key to success. Discuss options and come up with the best possible plan for the situation you are faced with.

Key Points

- Without proper planning your objective is destined to fail.

- Use a specific format when planning.

- Simplicity is a key to success.

- Gather intelligence beforehand.

Chapter 19 Deal with a True Threat—Stress

> *The general must avail himself of any helpful circumstances over and beyond the ordinary rules.*
>
> —Sun Tzu (Giles)

Being a police officer is considered one of the most stressful jobs you can have, with the possible exception of our military members in a combat zone. You would be hard-pressed to find a civilian job that generates as much real life and death stress on a regular basis as that of a law enforcement officer. The job of being an American law enforcement officer ranks within the top ten on most lists of stressful jobs and, in the majority of these lists, it is often ranked in the top five. Other jobs have their moments of intense stress for brief periods of time such as a doctor in an emergency operating room, a firefighter actually fighting a fire or even a lawyer in court, but the officers on the streets have to deal with a certain level of stress everyday on every call. The stress you can experience as a law enforcement officer can come from many different sources. Each stressor can affect you in a different way and take a toll on you if you are unprepared for it.

Stress is actually the body's reaction to any change that requires an adjustment or a response to a stimulus. Stress in police work comes in many forms and from many different sources. However, I will separate most forms of stress into two categories, which I will refer to as Performance Stress and Emotional Stress.

Performance Stress describes the body's reactions physically when having to perform under stressful and possibly life-threatening conditions. Emotional Stress deals with the psychological reactions that occur during and after a stressful situation. Emotional Stress is the focus of this chapter. Performance Stress is discussed throughout the book, especially in areas dealing with training.

I have broken down what I refer to as Emotional Stress into two categories: External and Internal. An example of External Emotional Stress is constantly dealing with complaining citizens, getting yelled at by irate people, dealing with hard-core criminals and, of course, the ever-present danger of being injured or killed. This external stress encompasses all of the emotional stress that comes from outside of your agency. The Internal emotional stress of police work comes from within your agency in dealing with your immediate supervisor, worrying about how the Administration will handle a citizen complaint, whether you can get a day off approved or if you are going to get held over after a 12-hour shift because someone called in sick. You will have to deal with both forms of emotional stress on a daily basis.

Another important aspect of Internal stress is what an officer deals with at home before and after work. There are all sorts of additional stressors officers have to deal with off-duty that can affect them while on-duty. Can I get the kids to school on time? Will I get off-duty in time to take them to practice? Did I pay my mortgage on time? Am I in debt? Can I get enough sleep before my next 12-hour shift? Am I spending quality time with my family? Plus the hundred or so other routine items that cause stress in the everyday world. Sometimes while off-duty you will feel like you are on-duty 24 hours a day because you need to check e-mails, return calls, complete projects, worry about ongoing cases and then have to go to court or attend training sessions on your days off. When work takes over you forget about everything else, including family.

It is important to recognize that you will be exposed to some sort of stress your entire career and you need to prepare yourself for that. Some people over time simply realize they cannot take the pressures of this job, but the better you prepare yourself the easier it will be for you to make it to retirement and beyond.

An especially scary aspect of the effect of stress of police work is the suicide rate among officers. According to The Badge of Life Organization, which is a suicide prevention program, there were 108 police suicides in 2016, which indicates there was one police suicide every 81 hours. During that same year only 97 officers died from gunshots and accidents combined. This is not quite as high as the military suicide rate, which at one point was averaging 22 suicides every day. However, there are close to 22 million veterans in the United States compared to 600,000 law enforcement officers.

It is important to help others and recognize the effects of excessive negative stress. For every suicide that occurs there are over 1,000 officers suffering with some aspect of stress. This stress is usually associated with a traumatic or critical incident that involved the officer. This condition is Post Traumatic Stress Disorder (PTSD). If early signs of PTSD are not recognized and treated, the stress can become a serious issue for the officer involved. Many departments are now including a mental health check-up for their officers on a regular basis, which is a positive change and should become the norm for all agencies.

Do not think that suicide happens to officers only in other departments. My agency was touched by a suicide involving an officer from a neighboring agency. Our department allows agencies to supply officers to our SWAT Team to form a regional response team. One of these officers that I had trained with for several years was involved in a pending divorce. During a heated argument with his wife he attacked and strangled her. He thought he had killed her when she went unconscious so he fled her residence. When the incident was reported to the local police his description was broadcast to other neighboring agencies. He was eventually contacted by the police when he arrived at his home. After a lengthy standoff he put a gun to his head and killed himself.

You have to wonder what kind of stress he was going through that could have lead up to this tragic event. You also have to think of what could have been done to recognize the issues to have helped him and his family.

Other warning signs that an officer may be suffering from a high level of stress would be alcoholism, substance abuse, financial crisis and gambling addictions to name a few indicators.

One myth that I always thought to be true was that the divorce rate among officers would be higher than other professions because of all the stress of the job. Interestingly enough, a recent study by Radcliffe University showed that the law enforcement divorce rate was close to 14%, which is lower than the national average of 16%. The jobs with the highest divorce rates were dancers at 43% and bartenders at 38%.

I could write an entire book on the subject of stress in law enforcement, but many people have done that before me. An excellent book on the subject of emotional stress that I highly recommend every police officer and spouse read is Kevin Gilmartin's book, *Emotional Survival for Law Enforcement—A Guide for Officers and Their Families.* Gilmartin describes the emotional roller-coaster that officers are on between on- and off-duty and their states of hypervigilance. Gilmartin states, "hypervigilance is the necessary manner of viewing the world from a threat-based perspective, having the mindset to see the events unfolding as potentially hazardous." This state can save your lifer, but it is hard to live that way 24/7. He also provides insights into strategies on how to survive a career in law enforcement and balance your job with the rest of your life. This book is a MUST read.

It is important to be aware of the effects of emotional stress because it is an enemy that we all have to fight, and sometimes it's a battle we fight on our own with little or no backup. Sun Tzu understood that we have to do everything we can to avoid defeat from any type of enemy, including stress, when he said, ***To secure ourselves against defeat lies in our own hands.*** Thus, it is important you recognize the effects of stress on both you and the ones you care about.

I want to talk about a few of my experiences during my career in the hope they will provide you some guidance in dealing with your own emotional stress. There have been several incidents that have caused me a high levels of stress but in different ways.

The first situation I want to mention has actually happened to me twice, and it is something I would never wish on anyone. In both of these incidents I was dispatched to calls of infants not breathing. One child died of SIDS (Sudden Infant Death Syndrome) and the other died from aspirating some vomit while sleeping. I was first on scene to both calls and immediately started CPR and carried them out to the arriving ambulance. Dealing with helpless infants is something that brings on its own level of stress. I still think about those two calls even though they happened early in my career in the 1990s.

After the ambulance arrived on scene during the first incident and I turned the child over to the paramedics, I followed them to the hospital. I was present when the young parents arrived and were notified their young infant had died. They started blaming me for not doing more to save their child. That was hard for me in itself, but I understood their frustration. They were just lashing out. I still had to conduct my investigation into the death while I was at the hospital. When the Coroner arrived, I left the parents and went with him so he could examine the deceased baby who was still in an examine room. With no warning at all he stuck a needle into the eye of the baby to get a fluid sample to determine the time of death. I had no idea that this was how it was done and, believe me, I was not ready for that procedure. We then left the hospital and I followed the coroner to the parents' residence. (By the way, the Coroner just wrapped the baby in a blanket and placed it on the floorboard behind his seat because he did not want to call the coroner's wagon.) The incident occurred early in the morning and when I finished with the investigation it was around noon. My Sergeant expected me to continue with my shift for another four hours. I certainly was not in an effective state of mind for those last four hours and definitely did not sleep well that night. During the call, and long afterward, I experienced waves of emotions from anger, frustration, helplessness and complete sadness.

This first incident occurred early in my career when my department did not have a Critical Incident Team and officers were expected to just suck it up and carry on. Cops were not to show emotion or weakness. (Note to supervisors: Check on your people after calls like this. A simple "Are you OK?" can go a long way.)

Fortunately, times have changed since that first incident. The majority of departments are now more understanding and recognize the emotional toll critical incidents take on the officers involved.

On the second incident involving the death of an infant I was given the opportunity to take the rest of the day off to decompress. The incident had involved a young infant that had been ill and drowned in its sleep on its own vomit. Kevin Dolezal, an officer I greatly respect and had worked with for many years, took the time to talk with me and later called me at home to see how I was doing. Kevin had been at the hospital with me and the call also affected him greatly. He had arrived at the hospital just in time to see a large medical gurney with a blanket covering a small mound in the middle being wheeled out of the Emergency

Room. A few days later I attended a debriefing about the incident along with Kevin, some other officers that were there, all the medical personnel that responded including some firefighters and our dispatchers. It is important for me to mention that the dispatcher who sent me to this call was my wife who, at the time, was pregnant with our first child. This one call affected all of us deeply and it took a long time to recover from it. Being able to openly talk about my feelings during the debriefing with fellow officers who understood where I was coming from and were familiar with the incident was a big help in getting through it all. However, the call from Kevin was the best therapy I could have received. It was a show of genuine concern and not something he was forced to do.

A third incident I want to mention occurred in early 2005. A deranged, mentally disturbed subject had assaulted several family members and then barricaded himself in his bedroom. He armed himself with a machete and a homemade spear and refused to surrender or comply with the responding officers. Our SWAT Team was eventually activated after a prolonged standoff to help resolve the situation and that is when I got involved. After our arrival, we removed the exterior window to the bedroom in which the subject was barricaded and attempted to negotiate with him. He retreated into the closet and refused to come out. However, he eventually burst from the closet and rushed at the open window where I was standing along with another officer. He crossed the distance of the small bedroom in what seemed like milliseconds. He was still armed with his spear and machete and posed an obvious threat if he got to us. (It is amazing how big a machete looks coming at you.) We were compelled to use deadly force and had to shoot the subject several times to stop him from exiting the bedroom window and landing on his feet in the yard where he could have inflicted some serious injuries. There would also have been a serious cross-fire situation if he had managed to land between the officers stationed at the window. The entire use-of-force portion of the incident occurred in what seemed like a split second from the moment he charged to when I was forced to fire to when he came to rest at my feet.

The level and types of stress I experienced that night were 180 degrees different from the first two incidents involving children. The date, time, location, and every detail of the event in which I was forced to use deadly force for the first time is seared into my memory more than any other event in my life. I experienced the full range of the physiological effects associated with being in a life-threatening situation, such as time distortion, tunnel vision and auditory exclusion. The M-4 rifle being fired in full auto bursts right next to me sounded like quiet pops. All I could see was the machete in his hand getting closer. I had a mini-time warp occurrence in which the incident sped up and then slowed down at critical moments. It was only as the speed of the incident returned to normal that I remember firing my last round. I was told I fired at least five rounds. It was not until a few minutes after the event, when the scene was secured, that I had a massive adrenaline dump. At that point, what had just occurred really started to set in. It was then that I started to second guess my actions, wondering if I had done the right thing, even though I knew I had.

Soon after the shooting I was paired up with another SWAT officer who had been on scene but had not fired. He drove me back to the police department as part of the investigation. While there I was separated from the other two officers that had also fired their weapons. I was asked to sit in a room and wait to be interviewed, but I had to get up and walk around. The adrenaline was still surging and it took quite a while to actually calm down.

I was allowed to call my wife to let her know what had happened and that I was OK, which helped calm me down (I'm not sure what it did to her). In our agency, as in most others, if we are involved in a critical incident we will have an officer assigned to stay with us to make sure we are OK. We can choose who we want and I asked for Kevin Dolezal, the same officer that was with me at one of the infant's deaths. He immediately responded to the station. I believe that having an officer to talk to who understands what you are going through is more helpful than any counselor or psychiatrist. Kevin had also been involved in his own shooting incident several years prior and understood better than most what I was experiencing.

Being able to talk openly about your experiences without being judged is an important aspect of dealing with traumatic situations. It may not prevent the effects of Post Traumatic Stress Disorder (PTSD), but it surely helps.

I believe that Sun Tzu's principle of ***creating a helpful situation over and beyond ordinary rules*** applies here. Officers and supervisors need to do more to look out for each other and check on their well-being. We understand better than anyone else what it is we experience on the street, so we are in the best position to help. On many occasions we might actually be involved in the incident ourselves and see the event firsthand. Because of this experience, it is important to know the same incident can affect everyone involved in different ways, which applies to all professions when it comes to dealing with stress. In law enforcement we need to look out for ourselves because we are the ones that have an intimate knowledge of what is going on. Unless you have been there yourself, how can you really know what it was like? Doctors and therapists can diagnose your condition and provide some treatment options, but can they really sit there and tell you they understand? How could they? To actually open up and talk about your feelings you need to trust the person you are talking to and that trust needs to be earned.

It is, therefore, up to us to look out for each other, especially if you are a senior officer or an immediate supervisor. It will mean more to an officer involved in a critical incident to have the support of his peers than that of the Chief or the Administration, not that that is not appreciated. I have seen several incidents where Administrators showed up and said a few words because they felt obligated to. You could see and feel the lack of sincerity and true caring a mile away. I will always remember when my mother passed away. My Chief at the time sent me a short text message the next day. He never took the time to call me directly and never said anything to me in person when I returned to work.

Sun Tzu understood the importance of knowing yourself and the people (soldiers) you work with when he wrote, **Carefully study the well-being of your men and do not overtax them.** By recognizing what can cause emotional stress in our jobs and developing strategies to deal with it when it does happen, we are preparing ourselves to get through both the incident and our careers intact. We also need to watch out for our fellow officers and not be afraid to intervene and offer help when the officer involved is not willing to ask himself.

Key Points

- Recognize the causes and symptoms of stress.

- Plan to deal with stress before a critical incident.

- Watch out for yourself and fellow officers and get help if needed.

- Read the book Emotional Survival for Police.

CONCLUSION

Now that you have spent some time reading and learning about Sun Tzu I hope you can appreciate the significance of *The Art of War*, especially when you consider it was written 2,500 years ago. When I was first introduced to the book, I could tell that it was worth reading, and it was definitely worth taking the time to study to have a basic understanding of Sun Tzu's principles and how they related to warfare.

It took me much longer to realize that these same principles could be used in law enforcement. When I began instructing officers in various topics, I always tried to keep up-to-date on current trends and procedures. Oddly enough, some of the quotes I kept seeing in training articles where from Sun Tzu. Now I understand why his work has been so influential.

My background comes from a few years serving in the US Army and quite a few more years working as a law enforcement patrol officer. My interpretations of Sun Tzu's maxims are based solely on my own experiences, training and understanding of *The Art of War*, which may differ greatly from the work of scholars with advanced degrees in ancient civilizations, philosophies and military history.

But I think that is the whole point of Sun Tzu's book and the way he would have wanted it—to read and interpret his teachings and apply it to the environment you may find yourself operating in. If you take the time to read *The Art of War*, your understanding and interpretations may end up being different than mine, or you may find they apply differently to situations that I have not addressed in my book. However, the underlying meaning of his maxims will still apply.

I fully understand anyone having his or her own take on Sun Tzu's book, because the important aspect of all of this is that we are thinking about how we can better our chances of survival. *The Art of War* is just another tool we can use to help better ourselves and the people we work with.

My intent for writing this book was to give the reader a resource to *The Art of War* and make it a "thought producer" for the reader to have a successful and safe career. I feel this knowledge will greatly enhance your officer safety training and, therefore, your outlook on your chosen profession of law enforcement. This will do nothing but make you better prepared to survive.

And this is important because,

> The Art of War *teaches us to rely not on*
> *the likelihood of the enemy not coming,*
> *but on our own readiness to receive him.*

> *—Sun Tzu , 500 BC*

SUN TZU ON THE ART OF WAR

THE OLDEST MILITARY TREATISE
IN THE WORLD
孫子兵法
Translated from the Chinese
By LIONEL GILES, M.A. (1910)

I.   LAYING PLANS

1. Sun Tzu said: The art of war is of vital importance to the State.

2. It is a matter of life and death, a road either to safety or to ruin. Hence it is subject of inquiry which can on no account be neglected.

3. The art of war, then, is governed by five constant factors, to be taken into account in one's deliberations, when seeking to determine the conditions obtaining in the field.

4. These are: (1) The Moral Law; (2) Heaven; (3) Earth; (4) The Commander; (5) Method and discipline.

5,6. The Moral Law causes the people to be in complete accord with their ruler, so that they will follow him regardless of their lives, undismayed by any danger.

7. Heaven signifies night and day, cold and heat, times and seasons.

8. Earth comprises distances, great and small; danger and security; open ground and narrow passes; the chances of life and death.

9. The Commander stands for the virtues of wisdom, sincerely, benevolence, courage and strictness.

10. By method and discipline are to be understood the marshaling of the army in its proper subdivisions, the graduations of rank among

the officers, the maintenance of roads by which supplies may reach the army, and the control of military expenditure.

11. These five heads should be familiar to every general: he who knows them will be victorious; he who knows them not will fail.

12. Therefore, in your deliberations, when seeking to determine the military conditions, let them be made the basis of a comparison, in this wise:—

13. (1) Which of the two sovereigns is imbued with the Moral law?
    (2) Which of the two generals has most ability?
    (3) With whom lie the advantages derived from Heaven and Earth?
    (4) On which side is discipline most rigorously enforced?
    (5) Which army is stronger?
    (6) On which side are officers and men more highly trained?
    (7) In which army is there the greater constancy both in reward and punishment?

14. By means of these seven considerations I can forecast victory or defeat.

15. The general that hearkens to my counsel and acts upon it, will conquer: let such a one be retained in command! The general that hearkens not to my counsel nor acts upon it, will suffer defeat:—let such a one be dismissed!

16. While heading the profit of my counsel, avail yourself also of any helpful circumstances over and beyond the ordinary rules.

17. According as circumstances are favorable, one should modify one's plans.

18. All warfare is based on deception.

19. Hence, when able to attack, we must seem unable; when using our forces, we must seem inactive; when we are near, we must make the enemy believe we are far away; when far away, we must make him believe we are near.

20. Hold out baits to entice the enemy. Feign disorder, and crush him.

21. If he is secure at all points, be prepared for him. If he is in superior strength, evade him.

22. If your opponent is of choleric temper, seek to irritate him. Pretend to be weak, that he may grow arrogant.

23. If he is taking his ease, give him no rest. If his forces are united, separate them.

24. Attack him where he is unprepared, appear where you are not expected.

25. These military devices, leading to victory, must not be divulged beforehand.

26. Now the general who wins a battle makes many calculations in his temple before the battle is fought. The general who loses a battle makes but few calculations beforehand. Thus, many calculations lead to victory, and few calculations to defeat: how much more no calculation at all! It is by attention to this point that I can foresee who is likely to win or lose.

II.   WAGING WAR

1. Sun Tzu said: In the operations of war, where there are in the field a thousand swift chariots, as many heavy chariots, and a hundred thousand mail-clad soldiers, with provisions enough to carry them a thousand li, the expenditure at home and at the front, including entertainment of guests, small items such as glue and paint, and sums spent on chariots and armor, will reach the total of a thousand ounces of silver per day. Such is the cost of raising an army of 100,000 men.

2. When you engage in actual fighting, if victory is long in coming, then men' s weapons will grow dull and their ardor will be damped. If you lay siege to a town, you will exhaust your strength.

3. Again, if the campaign is protracted, the resources of the State will not be equal to the strain.

4. Now, when your weapons are dulled, your ardor damped, your strength exhausted and your treasure spent, other chieftains will spring up to take advantage of your extremity. Then no man, however wise, will be able to avert the consequences that must ensue.

5. Thus, though we have heard of stupid haste in war, cleverness has never been seen associated with long delays.

6. There is no instance of a country having benefited from prolonged warfare.

7. It is only one who is thoroughly acquainted with the evils of war that can thoroughly understand the profitable way of carrying it on.

8. The skillful soldier does not raise a second levy, neither are his supply-wagons loaded more than twice.

9. Bring war material with you from home, but forage on the enemy. Thus the army will have food enough for its needs.

10. Poverty of the State exchequer causes an army to be maintained by contributions from a distance. Contributing to maintain an army at a distance causes the people to be impoverished.

11. On the other hand, the proximity of an army causes prices to go up; and high prices cause the people's substance to be drained away.

12. When their substance is drained away, the peasantry will be afflicted by heavy exactions.

13,14. With this loss of substance and exhaustion of strength, the homes of the people will be stripped bare, and three-tenths of their income will be dissipated; while government expenses for broken chariots, worn-out horses, breast-plates and helmets, bows and arrows, spears and shields, protective mantles, draught-oxen and heavy wagons, will amount to four-tenths of its total revenue.

15. Hence a wise general makes a point of foraging on the enemy. One cartload of the enemy's provisions is equivalent to twenty of one's own, and likewise a single picul of his provender is equivalent to twenty from one's own store.

16. Now in order to kill the enemy, our men must be roused to anger; that there may be advantage from defeating the enemy, they must have their rewards.

17. Therefore, in chariot fighting, when ten or more chariots have been taken, those should be rewarded who took the first. Our own flags should be substituted for those of the enemy, and the chariots mingled and used in conjunction with ours. The captured soldiers should be kindly treated and kept.

18. This is called, using the conquered foe to augment one's own strength.

19. In war, then, let your great object be victory, not lengthy campaigns.

20. Thus it may be known that the leader of armies is the arbiter of the people's fate, the man on whom it depends whether the nation shall be in peace or in peril.

III.   ATTACK BY STRATAGEM

1. Sun Tzu said: In the practical art of war, the best thing of all is to take the enemy's country whole and intact; to shatter and destroy it is not so good. So, too, it is better to recapture an army entire than to destroy it, to capture a regiment, a detachment or a company entire than to destroy them.

2. Hence to fight and conquer in all your battles is not supreme excellence; supreme excellence consists in breaking the enemy's resistance without fighting.

3. Thus the highest form of generalship is to balk the enemy's plans; the next best is to prevent the junction of the enemy's forces; the next in order is to attack the enemy's army in the field; and the worst policy of all is to besiege walled cities.

4. The rule is, not to besiege walled cities if it can possibly be avoided. The preparation of mantlets, movable shelters, and various implements of war, will take up three whole months; and the piling up of mounds over against the walls will take three months more.

5. The general, unable to control his irritation, will launch his men to the assault like swarming ants, with the result that one-third of his men are slain, while the town still remains untaken. Such are the disastrous effects of a siege.

6. Therefore, the skillful leader subdues the enemy's troops without any fighting; he captures their cities without laying siege to them; he overthrows their kingdom without lengthy operations in the field.

7. With his forces intact he will dispute the mastery of the Empire, and thus, without losing a man, his triumph will be complete. This is the method of attacking by stratagem.

8. It is the rule in war, if our forces are ten to the enemy's one, to surround him; if five to one, to attack him; if twice as numerous, to divide our army into two.

9. If equally matched, we can offer battle; if slightly inferior in numbers, we can avoid the enemy; if quite unequal in every way, we can flee from him.

10. Hence, though an obstinate fight may be made by a small force, in the end it must be captured by the larger force.

11. Now the general is the bulwark of the State; if the bulwark is complete at all points; the State will be strong; if the bulwark is defective, the State will be weak.

12. There are three ways in which a ruler can bring misfortune upon his army:—

13. (1) By commanding the army to advance or to retreat, being ignorant of the fact that it cannot obey. This is called hobbling the army.

14. (2) By attempting to govern an army in the same way as he administers a kingdom, being ignorant of the conditions which obtain in an army. This causes restlessness in the soldier's minds.

15. (3) By employing the officers of his army without discrimination, through ignorance of the military principle of adaptation to circumstances. This shakes the confidence of the soldiers.

16. But when the army is restless and distrustful, trouble is sure to come from the other feudal princes. This is simply bringing anarchy into the army, and flinging victory away.

17. Thus we may know that there are five essentials for victory:
    (1) He will win who knows when to fight and when not to fight.
    (2) He will win who knows how to handle both superior and inferior forces.
    (3) He will win whose army is animated by the same spirit throughout all its ranks.
    (4) He will win who, prepared himself, waits to take the enemy unprepared.
    (5) He will win who has military capacity and is not interfered with by the sovereign.

18. Hence the saying: If you know the enemy and know yourself, you need not fear the result of a hundred battles. If you know yourself but not the enemy, for every victory gained you will also suffer a defeat. If you know neither the enemy nor yourself, you will succumb in every battle.

IV.   TACTICAL DISPOSITIONS

1. Sun Tzu said: The good fighters of old first put themselves beyond the possibility of defeat, and then waited for an opportunity of defeating the enemy.

2. To secure ourselves against defeat lies in our own hands, but the opportunity of defeating the enemy is provided by the enemy himself.

3. Thus the good fighter is able to secure himself against defeat, but cannot make certain of defeating the enemy.

4. Hence the saying: One may know how to conquer without being able to do it.

5. Security against defeat implies defensive tactics; ability to defeat the enemy means taking the offensive.

6. Standing on the defensive indicates insufficient strength; attacking, a superabundance of strength.

7. The general who is skilled in defense hides in the most secret recesses of the earth; he who is skilled in attack flashes forth from the topmost heights of heaven. Thus on the one hand we have ability to protect ourselves; on the other, a victory that is complete.

8. To see victory only when it is within the ken of the common herd is not the acme of excellence.

9. Neither is it the acme of excellence if you fight and conquer and the whole Empire says, "Well done!"

10. To lift an autumn hair is no sign of great strength; to see the sun and moon is no sign of sharp sight; to hear the noise of thunder is no sign of a quick ear.

11. What the ancients called a clever fighter is one who not only wins, but excels in winning with ease.

12. Hence his victories bring him neither reputation for wisdom nor credit for courage.

13. He wins his battles by making no mistakes. Making no mistakes is what establishes the certainty of victory, for it means conquering an enemy that is already defeated.

14. Hence the skillful fighter puts himself into a position which makes defeat impossible, and does not miss the moment for defeating the enemy.

15. Thus it is that in war the victorious strategist only seeks battle after the victory has been won, whereas he who is destined to defeat first fights and afterwards looks for victory.

16. The consummate leader cultivates the moral law, and strictly adheres to method and discipline; thus it is in his power to control success.

17. In respect of military method, we have, firstly, Measurement; secondly, Estimation of quantity; thirdly, Calculation; fourthly, Balancing of chances; fifthly, Victory.

18. Measurement owes its existence to Earth; Estimation of quantity to Measurement; Calculation to Estimation of quantity; Balancing of chances to Calculation; and Victory to Balancing of chances.

19. A victorious army opposed to a routed one, is as a pound's weight placed in the scale against a single grain.

20. The onrush of a conquering force is like the bursting of pent-up waters into a chasm a thousand fathoms deep.

V.   ENERGY

1. Sun Tzu said: The control of a large force is the same principle as the control of a few men: it is merely a question of dividing up their numbers.

2. Fighting with a large army under your command is nowise different from fighting with a small one: it is merely a question of instituting signs and signals.

3. To ensure that your whole host may withstand the brunt of the enemy's attack and remain unshaken—this is effected by maneuvers direct and indirect.

4. That the impact of your army may be like a grindstone dashed against an egg—this is effected by the science of weak points and strong.

5. In all fighting, the direct method may be used for joining battle, but indirect methods will be needed in order to secure victory.

6. Indirect tactics, efficiently applied, are inexhaustible as Heaven and Earth, unending as the flow of rivers and streams; like the sun and moon, they end but to begin anew; like the four seasons, they pass away to return once more.

7. There are not more than five musical notes, yet the combinations of these five give rise to more melodies than can ever be heard.

8. There are not more than five primary colors (blue, yellow, red, white, and black), yet in combination they produce more hues than can ever been seen.

9. There are not more than five cardinal tastes (sour, acrid, salt, sweet, bitter), yet combinations of them yield more flavors than can ever be tasted.

10. In battle, there are not more than two methods of attack—the direct and the indirect; yet these two in combination give rise to an endless series of maneuvers.

11. The direct and the indirect lead on to each other in turn. It is like moving in a circle—you never come to an end. Who can exhaust the possibilities of their combination?

12. The onset of troops is like the rush of a torrent which will even roll stones along in its course.

13. The quality of decision is like the well-timed swoop of a falcon which enables it to strike and destroy its victim.

14. Therefore, the good fighter will be terrible in his onset, and prompt in his decision.

15. Energy may be likened to the bending of a crossbow; decision, to the releasing of a trigger.

16. Amid the turmoil and tumult of battle, there may be seeming disorder and yet no real disorder at all; amid confusion and chaos, your array may be without head or tail, yet it will be proof against defeat.

17. Simulated disorder postulates perfect discipline, simulated fear postulates courage; simulated weakness postulates strength.

18. Hiding order beneath the cloak of disorder is simply a question of subdivision; concealing courage under a show of timidity presupposes a fund of latent energy; masking strength with weakness is to be effected by tactical dispositions.

19. Thus one who is skillful at keeping the enemy on the move maintains deceitful appearances, according to which the enemy will act. He sacrifices something, that the enemy may snatch at it.

20. By holding out baits, he keeps him on the march; then with a body of picked men he lies in wait for him.

21. The clever combatant looks to the effect of combined energy, and does not require too much from individuals. Hence his ability to pick out the right men and utilize combined energy.

22. When he utilizes combined energy, his fighting men become as it were like unto rolling logs or stones. For it is the nature of a log or stone to remain motionless on level ground, and to move when on

a slope; if four-cornered, to come to a standstill, but if round-shaped, to go rolling down.

23. Thus the energy developed by good fighting men is as the momentum of a round stone rolled down a mountain thousands of feet in height. So much on the subject of energy.

VI.   WEAK POINTS AND STRONG

1. Sun Tzu said: Whoever is first in the field and awaits the coming of the enemy, will be fresh for the fight; whoever is second in the field and has to hasten to battle will arrive exhausted.

2. Therefore, the clever combatant imposes his will on the enemy, but does not allow the enemy's will to be imposed on him.

3. By holding out advantages to him, he can cause the enemy to approach of his own accord; or, by inflicting damage, he can make it impossible for the enemy to draw near.

4. If the enemy is taking his ease, he can harass him; if well supplied with food, he can starve him out; if quietly encamped, he can force him to move.

5. Appear at points which the enemy must hasten to defend; march swiftly to places where you are not expected.

6. An army may march great distances without distress, if it marches through country where the enemy is not.

7. You can be sure of succeeding in your attacks if you only attack places which are undefended. You can ensure the safety of your defense if you only hold positions that cannot be attacked.

8. Hence that general is skillful in attack whose opponent does not know what to defend; and he is skillful in defense whose opponent does not know what to attack.

9. O divine art of subtlety and secrecy! Through you we learn to be invisible, through you inaudible; and hence we can hold the enemy's fate in our hands.

10. You may advance and be absolutely irresistible, if you make for the enemy's weak points; you may retire and be safe from pursuit if your movements are more rapid than those of the enemy.

11. If we wish to fight, the enemy can be forced to an engagement even though he be sheltered behind a high rampart and a deep ditch. All we need do is attack some other place that he will be obliged to relieve.

12. If we do not wish to fight, we can prevent the enemy from engaging us even though the lines of our encampment be merely traced out on the ground. All we need do is to throw something odd and unaccountable in his way.

13. By discovering the enemy's dispositions and remaining invisible ourselves, we can keep our forces concentrated, while the enemy's must be divided.

14. We can form a single united body, while the enemy must split up into fractions. Hence there will be a whole pitted against separate parts of a whole, which means that we shall be many to the enemy's few.

15. And if we are able thus to attack an inferior force with a superior one, our opponents will be in dire straits.

16. The spot where we intend to fight must not be made known; for then the enemy will have to prepare against a possible attack at several different points; and his forces being thus distributed in many directions, the numbers we shall have to face at any given point will be proportionately few.

17. For should the enemy strengthen his van, he will weaken his rear; should he strengthen his rear, he will weaken his van; should he strengthen his left, he will weaken his right; should he strengthen

his right, he will weaken his left. If he sends reinforcements every-where, he will everywhere be weak.

18. Numerical weakness comes from having to prepare against possi-ble attacks; numerical strength, from compelling our adversary to make these preparations against us.

19. Knowing the place and the time of the coming battle, we may concentrate from the greatest distances in order to fight.

20. But if neither time nor place be known, then the left wing will be impotent to succor the right, the right equally impotent to succor the left, the van unable to relieve the rear, or the rear to support the van. How much more so if the furthest portions of the army are anything under a hundred LI apart, and even the nearest are separated by several LI!

21. Though according to my estimate the soldiers of Yueh exceed our own in number, that shall advantage them nothing in the matter of victory. I say then that victory can be achieved.

22. Though the enemy be stronger in numbers, we may prevent him from fighting. Scheme so as to discover his plans and the likelihood of their success.

23. Rouse him, and learn the principle of his activity or inactivity. Force him to reveal himself, so as to find out his vulnerable spots.

24. Carefully compare the opposing army with your own, so that you may know where strength is superabundant and where it is deficient.

25. In making tactical dispositions, the highest pitch you can attain is to conceal them; conceal your dispositions, and you will be safe from the prying of the subtlest spies, from the machinations of the wisest brains.

26. How victory may be produced for them out of the enemy's own tactics—that is what the multitude cannot comprehend.

27. All men can see the tactics whereby I conquer, but what none can see is the strategy out of which victory is evolved.

28. Do not repeat the tactics which have gained you one victory, but let your methods be regulated by the infinite variety of circumstances.

29. Military tactics are like unto water; for water in its natural course runs away from high places and hastens downwards.

30. So in war, the way is to avoid what is strong and to strike at what is weak.

31. Water shapes its course according to the nature of the ground over which it flows; the soldier works out his victory in relation to the foe whom he is facing.

32. Therefore, just as water retains no constant shape, so in warfare there are no constant conditions.

33. He who can modify his tactics in relation to his opponent and thereby succeed in winning, may be called a heaven-born captain.

34. The five elements (water, fire, wood, metal, earth) are not always equally predominant; the four seasons make way for each other in turn. There are short days and long; the moon has its periods of waning and waxing.

VII.   MANEUVERING

1. Sun Tzu said: In war, the general receives his commands from the sovereign.

2. Having collected an army and concentrated his forces, he must blend and harmonize the different elements there of before pitching his camp.

3. After that, comes tactical maneuvering, than which there is nothing more difficult. The difficulty of tactical maneuvering consists in turning the devious into the direct, and misfortune into gain.

4. Thus, to take a long and circuitous route, after enticing the enemy out of the way, and though starting after him, to contrive to reach the goal before him, shows knowledge of the artifice of DEVIATION.

5. Maneuvering with an army is advantageous; with an undisciplined multitude, most dangerous.

6. If you set a fully equipped army in march in order to snatch an advantage, the chances are that you will be too late. On the other hand, to detach a flying column for the purpose involves the sacrifice of its baggage and stores.

7. Thus, if you order your men to roll up their buff-coats, and make forced marches without halting day or night, covering double the usual distance at a stretch, doing a hundred LI in order to wrest an advantage, the leaders of all your three divisions will fall into the hands of the enemy.

8. The stronger men will be in front, the jaded ones will fall behind, and on this plan only one-tenth of your army will reach its destination.

9. If you march fifty LI in order to outmaneuver the enemy, you will lose the leader of your first division, and only half your force will reach the goal.

10. If you march thirty LI with the same object, two-thirds of your army will arrive.

11. We may take it then that an army without its baggage-train is lost; without provisions it is lost; without bases of supply it is lost.

12. We cannot enter into alliances until we are acquainted with the designs of our neighbors.

13. We are not fit to lead an army on the march unless we are familiar with the face of the country—its mountains and forests, its pitfalls and precipices, its marshes and swamps.

14. We shall be unable to turn natural advantage to account unless we make use of local guides.

15. In war, practice dissimulation, and you will succeed.

16. Whether to concentrate or to divide your troops, must be decided by circumstances.

17. Let your rapidity be that of the wind, your compactness that of the forest.

18. In raiding and plundering be like fire, is immovability like a mountain.

19. Let your plans be dark and impenetrable as night, and when you move, fall like a thunderbolt.

20. When you plunder a countryside, let the spoil be divided amongst your men; when you capture new territory, cut it up into allotments for the benefit of the soldiery.

21. Ponder and deliberate before you make a move.

22. He will conquer who has learnt the artifice of deviation. Such is the art of maneuvering.

23. The Book of Army Management says: On the field of battle, the spoken word does not carry far enough: hence the institution of gongs and drums. Nor can ordinary objects be seen clearly enough: hence the institution of banners and flags.

24. Gongs and drums, banners and flags, are means whereby the ears and eyes of the host may be focused on one particular point.

25. The host thus forming a single united body, is it impossible either for the brave to advance alone, or for the cowardly to retreat alone. This is the art of handling large masses of men.

26. In night-fighting, then, make much use of signal-fires and drums, and in fighting by day, of flags and banners, as a means of influencing the ears and eyes of your army.

27. A whole army may be robbed of its spirit; a commander-in-chief may be robbed of his presence of mind.

28. Now a soldier's spirit is keenest in the morning; by noonday it has begun to flag; and in the evening, his mind is bent only on returning to camp.

29. A clever general, therefore, avoids an army when its spirit is keen, but attacks it when it is sluggish and inclined to return. This is the art of studying moods.

30. Disciplined and calm, to await the appearance of disorder and hubbub amongst the enemy:—this is the art of retaining self-possession.

31. To be near the goal while the enemy is still far from it, to wait at ease while the enemy is toiling and struggling, to be well-fed while the enemy is famished:—this is the art of husbanding one's strength.

32. To refrain from intercepting an enemy whose banners are in perfect order, to refrain from attacking an army drawn up in calm and confident array:—this is the art of studying circumstances.

33. It is a military axiom not to advance uphill against the enemy, nor to oppose him when he comes downhill.

34. Do not pursue an enemy who simulates flight; do not attack soldiers whose temper is keen.

35. Do not swallow bait offered by the enemy. Do not interfere with an army that is returning home.

36. When you surround an army, leave an outlet free. Do not press a desperate foe too hard.

37. Such is the art of warfare.

VIII.   VARIATION IN TACTICS

1. Sun Tzu said: In war, the general receives his commands from the sovereign, collects his army and concentrates his forces

2. When in difficult country, do not encamp. In country where high roads intersect, join hands with your allies. Do not linger in dangerously isolated positions. In hemmed-in situations, you must resort to stratagem. In desperate position, you must fight.

3. There are roads which must not be followed, armies which must be not attacked, towns which must be besieged, positions which must not be contested, commands of the sovereign which must not be obeyed.

4. The general who thoroughly understands the advantages that accompany variation of tactics knows how to handle his troops.

5. The general who does not understand these, may be well acquainted with the configuration of the country, yet he will not be able to turn his knowledge to practical account.

6. So, the student of war who is unversed in the art of war of varying his plans, even though he be acquainted with the Five Advantages, will fail to make the best use of his men.

7. Hence in the wise leader's plans, considerations of advantage and of disadvantage will be blended together.

8. If our expectation of advantage be tempered in this way, we may succeed in accomplishing the essential part of our schemes.

9. If, on the other hand, in the midst of difficulties we are always ready to seize an advantage, we may extricate ourselves from misfortune.

10. Reduce the hostile chiefs by inflicting damage on them; and make trouble for them, and keep them constantly engaged; hold out specious allurements, and make them rush to any given point.

11. The art of war teaches us to rely not on the likelihood of the enemy's not coming, but on our own readiness to receive him; not on the chance of his not attacking, but rather on the fact that we have made our position unassailable.

12. There are five dangerous faults which may affect a general:
    (1) Recklessness, which leads to destruction;
    (2) cowardice, which leads to capture;
    (3) a hasty temper, which can be provoked by insults;
    (4) a delicacy of honor which is sensitive to shame;
    (5) over-solicitude for his men, which exposes him to worry and trouble.

13. These are the five besetting sins of a general, ruinous to the conduct of war.

14. When an army is overthrown and its leader slain the cause will surely be found among these five dangerous faults. Let them be a subject of meditation.

IX.   THE ARMY ON THE MARCH

1. Sun Tzu said: We come now to the question of encamping the army, and observing signs of the enemy. Pass quickly over mountains, and keep in the neighborhood of valleys.

2. Camp in high places, facing the sun. Do not climb heights in order to fight. So much for mountain warfare.

3. After crossing a river, you should get far away from it.

4. When an invading force crosses a river in its onward march, do not advance to meet it in mid-stream. It will be best to let half the army get across, and then deliver your attack.

5. If you are anxious to fight, you should not go to meet the invader near a river which he has to cross.

6. Moor your craft higher up than the enemy, and facing the sun. Do not move up-stream to meet the enemy. So much for river warfare.

7. In crossing salt-marshes, your sole concern should be to get over them quickly, without any delay.

8. If forced to fight in a salt-marsh, you should have water and grass near you, and get your back to a clump of trees. So much for operations in salt-marches.

9. In dry, level country, take up an easily accessible position with rising ground to your right and on your rear, so that the danger may be in front, and safety lie behind. So much for campaigning in flat country.

10. These are the four useful branches of military knowledge which enabled the Yellow Emperor to vanquish four several sovereigns.

11. All armies prefer high ground to low and sunny places to dark.

12. If you are careful of your men, and camp on hard ground, the army will be free from disease of every kind, and this will spell victory.

13. When you come to a hill or a bank, occupy the sunny side, with the slope on your right rear. Thus you will at once act for the benefit of your soldiers and utilize the natural advantages of the ground.

14. When, in consequence of heavy rains up-country, a river which you wish to ford is swollen and flecked with foam, you must wait until it subsides.

15. Country in which there are precipitous cliffs with torrents running between, deep natural hollows, confined places, tangled thickets, quagmires and crevasses, should be left with all possible speed and not approached.

16. While we keep away from such places, we should get the enemy to approach them; while we face them, we should let the enemy have them on his rear.

17. If in the neighborhood of your camp there should be any hilly country, ponds surrounded by aquatic grass, hollow basins filled with reeds, or woods with thick undergrowth, they must be carefully routed out and searched; for these are places where men in ambush or insidious spies are likely to be lurking.

18. When the enemy is close at hand and remains quiet, he is relying on the natural strength of his position.

19. When he keeps aloof and tries to provoke a battle, he is anxious for the other side to advance.

20. If his place of encampment is easy of access, he is tendering a bait.

21. Movement amongst the trees of a forest shows that the enemy is advancing. The appearance of a number of screens in the midst of thick grass means that the enemy wants to make us suspicious.

22. The rising of birds in their flight is the sign of an ambuscade. Startled beasts indicate that a sudden attack is coming.

23. When there is dust rising in a high column, it is the sign of chariots advancing; when the dust is low, but spread over a wide area, it betokens the approach of infantry. When it branches out in different directions, it shows that parties have been sent to collect firewood. A few clouds of dust moving to and fro signify that the army is encamping.

24. Humble words and increased preparations are signs that the enemy is about to advance. Violent language and driving forward as if to the attack are signs that he will retreat.

25. When the light chariots come out first and take up a position on the wings, it is a sign that the enemy is forming for battle.

26. Peace proposals unaccompanied by a sworn covenant indicate a plot.

27. When there is much running about and the soldiers fall into rank, it means that the critical moment has come.

28. When some are seen advancing and some retreating, it is a lure.

29. When the soldiers stand leaning on their spears, they are faint from want of food.

30. If those who are sent to draw water begin by drinking themselves, the army is suffering from thirst.

31. If the enemy sees an advantage to be gained and makes no effort to secure it, the soldiers are exhausted.

32. If birds gather on any spot, it is unoccupied. Clamor by night betokens nervousness.

33. If there is disturbance in the camp, the general's authority is weak. If the banners and flags are shifted about, sedition is afoot. If the officers are angry, it means that the men are weary.

34. When an army feeds its horses with grain and kills its cattle for food, and when the men do not hang their cooking-pots over the camp-fires, showing that they will not return to their tents, you may know that they are determined to fight to the death.

35. The sight of men whispering together in small knots or speaking in subdued tones points to disaffection amongst the rank and file.

36. Too frequent rewards signify that the enemy is at the end of his resources; too many punishments betray a condition of dire distress.

37. To begin by bluster, but afterwards to take fright at the enemy's numbers, shows a supreme lack of intelligence.

38. When envoys are sent with compliments in their mouths, it is a sign that the enemy wishes for a truce.

39. If the enemy's troops march up angrily and remain facing ours for a long time without either joining battle or taking themselves off again, the situation is one that demands great vigilance and circumspection.

40. If our troops are no more in number than the enemy, that is amply sufficient; it only means that no direct attack can be made. What we can do is simply to concentrate all our available strength, keep a close watch on the enemy, and obtain reinforcements.

41. He who exercises no forethought but makes light of his opponents is sure to be captured by them.

42. If soldiers are punished before they have grown attached to you, they will not prove submissive; and, unless submissive, then will be practically useless. If, when the soldiers have become attached to you, punishments are not enforced, they will still be unless.

43. Therefore soldiers must be treated in the first instance with humanity, but kept under control by means of iron discipline. This is a certain road to victory.

44. If in training soldiers commands are habitually enforced, the army will be well-disciplined; if not, its discipline will be bad.

45. If a general shows confidence in his men but always insists on his orders being obeyed, the gain will be mutual.

X.   TERRAIN

1. Sun Tzu said: We may distinguish six kinds of terrain, to wit:
   (1) Accessible ground; (2) entangling ground; (3) temporizing
   ground; (4) narrow passes; (5) precipitous heights; (6) positions at
   a great distance from the enemy.

2. Ground which can be freely traversed by both sides is called
   accessible.

3. With regard to ground of this nature, be before the enemy in
   occupying the raised and sunny spots, and carefully guard your
   line of supplies. Then you will be able to fight with advantage.

4. Ground which can be abandoned but is hard to re-occupy is called
   entangling.

5. From a position of this sort, if the enemy is unprepared, you may
   sally forth and defeat him. But if the enemy is prepared for your
   coming, and you fail to defeat him, then, return being impossible,
   disaster will ensue.

6. When the position is such that neither side will gain by making the
   first move, it is called temporizing ground.

7. In a position of this sort, even though the enemy should offer us
   an attractive bait, it will be advisable not to stir forth, but rather to
   retreat, thus enticing the enemy in his turn; then, when part of his
   army has come out, we may deliver our attack with advantage.

8. With regard to narrow passes, if you can occupy them first, let
   them be strongly garrisoned and await the advent of the enemy.

9. Should the army forestall you in occupying a pass, do not go after
   him if the pass is fully garrisoned, but only if it is weakly
   garrisoned.

10. With regard to precipitous heights, if you are beforehand with
    your adversary, you should occupy the raised and sunny spots, and
    there wait for him to come up.

11. If the enemy has occupied them before you, do not follow him, but retreat and try to entice him away.

12. If you are situated at a great distance from the enemy, and the strength of the two armies is equal, it is not easy to provoke a battle, and fighting will be to your disadvantage.

13. These six are the principles connected with Earth. The general who has attained a responsible post must be careful to study them.

14. Now an army is exposed to six several calamities, not arising from natural causes, but from faults for which the general is responsible. These are: (1) Flight; (2) insubordination; (3) collapse; (4) ruin; (5) disorganization; (6) rout.

15. Other conditions being equal, if one force is hurled against another ten times its size, the result will be the flight of the former.

16. When the common soldiers are too strong and their officers too weak, the result is insubordination. When the officers are too strong and the common soldiers too weak, the result is collapse.

17. When the higher officers are angry and insubordinate, and on meeting the enemy give battle on their own account from a feeling of resentment, before the commander-in-chief can tell whether or no he is in a position to fight, the result is ruin.

18. When the general is weak and without authority; when his orders are not clear and distinct; when there are no fixes duties assigned to officers and men, and the ranks are formed in a slovenly haphazard manner, the result is utter disorganization.

19. When a general, unable to estimate the enemy's strength, allows an inferior force to engage a larger one, or hurls a weak detachment against a powerful one, and neglects to place picked soldiers in the front rank, the result must be rout.

20. These are six ways of courting defeat, which must be carefully noted by the general who has attained a responsible post.

21. The natural formation of the country is the soldier's best ally; but a power of estimating the adversary, of controlling the forces of victory, and of shrewdly calculating difficulties, dangers and distances, constitutes the test of a great general.

22. He who knows these things, and in fighting puts his knowledge into practice, will win his battles. He who knows them not, nor practices them, will surely be defeated.

23. If fighting is sure to result in victory, then you must fight, even though the ruler forbid it; if fighting will not result in victory, then you must not fight even at the ruler's bidding.

24. The general who advances without coveting fame and retreats without fearing disgrace, whose only thought is to protect his country and do good service for his sovereign, is the jewel of the kingdom.

25. Regard your soldiers as your children, and they will follow you into the deepest valleys; look upon them as your own beloved sons, and they will stand by you even unto death.

26. If, however, you are indulgent, but unable to make your authority felt; kind-hearted, but unable to enforce your commands; and incapable, moreover, of quelling disorder: then your soldiers must be likened to spoilt children; they are useless for any practical purpose.

27. If we know that our own men are in a condition to attack, but are unaware that the enemy is not open to attack, we have gone only halfway towards victory.

28. If we know that the enemy is open to attack, but are unaware that our own men are not in a condition to attack, we have gone only halfway towards victory.

29. If we know that the enemy is open to attack, and also know that our men are in a condition to attack, but are unaware that the nature of the ground makes fighting impracticable, we have still gone only halfway towards victory.

30. Hence the experienced soldier, once in motion, is never
bewildered; once he has broken camp, he is never at a loss.

31. Hence the saying: If you know the enemy and know yourself, your
victory will not stand in doubt; if you know Heaven and know
Earth, you may make your victory complete.

XI.   **THE NINE SITUATIONS**

1. Sun Tzu said: The art of war recognizes nine varieties of ground:
(1) Dispersive ground; (2) facile ground; (3) contentious ground;
(4) open ground; (5) ground of intersecting highways; (6) serious
ground; (7) difficult ground; (8) hemmed-in ground; (9) desperate
ground.

2. When a chieftain is fighting in his own territory, it is dispersive
ground.

3. When he has penetrated into hostile territory, but to no great
distance, it is facile ground.

4. Ground the possession of which imports great advantage to either
side, is contentious ground.

5. Ground on which each side has liberty of movement is open
ground.

6. Ground which forms the key to three contiguous states, so that he
who occupies it first has most of the Empire at his command, is a
ground of intersecting highways.

7. When an army has penetrated into the heart of a hostile country,
leaving a number of fortified cities in its rear, it is serious ground.

8. Mountain forests, rugged steeps, marshes and fens—all country
that is hard to traverse: this is difficult ground.

9. Ground which is reached through narrow gorges, and from which
we can only retire by tortuous paths, so that a small number of the

enemy would suffice to crush a large body of our men: this is hemmed in ground.

10. Ground on which we can only be saved from destruction by fighting without delay, is desperate ground.

11. On dispersive ground, therefore, fight not. On facile ground, halt not. On contentious ground, attack not.

12. On open ground, do not try to block the enemy's way. On the ground of intersecting highways, join hands with your allies.

13. On serious ground, gather in plunder. In difficult ground, keep steadily on the march.

14. On hemmed-in ground, resort to stratagem. On desperate ground, fight.

15. Those who were called skillful leaders of old knew how to drive a wedge between the enemy's front and rear; to prevent co-operation between his large and small divisions; to hinder the good troops from rescuing the bad, the officers from rallying their men.

16. When the enemy's men were united, they managed to keep them in disorder.

17. When it was to their advantage, they made a forward move; when otherwise, they stopped still.

18. If asked how to cope with a great host of the enemy in orderly array and on the point of marching to the attack, I should say: "Begin by seizing something which your opponent holds dear; then he will be amenable to your will."

19. Rapidity is the essence of war: take advantage of the enemy's unreadiness, make your way by unexpected routes, and attack unguarded spots.

20. The following are the principles to be observed by an invading force: The further you penetrate into a country, the greater will be

the solidarity of your troops, and thus the defenders will not prevail against you.

21. Make forays in fertile country in order to supply your army with food.

22. Carefully study the well-being of your men, and do not overtax them. Concentrate your energy and hoard your strength. Keep your army continually on the move, and devise unfathomable plans.

23. Throw your soldiers into positions whence there is no escape, and they will prefer death to flight. If they will face death, there is nothing they may not achieve. Officers and men alike will put forth their uttermost strength.

24. Soldiers when in desperate straits lose the sense of fear. If there is no place of refuge, they will stand firm. If they are in hostile country, they will show a stubborn front. If there is no help for it, they will fight hard.

25. Thus, without waiting to be marshaled, the soldiers will be constantly on the qui vive; without waiting to be asked, they will do your will; without restrictions, they will be faithful; without giving orders, they can be trusted.

26. Prohibit the taking of omens, and do away with superstitious doubts. Then, until death itself comes, no calamity need be feared.

27. If our soldiers are not overburdened with money, it is not because they have a distaste for riches; if their lives are not unduly long, it is not because they are disinclined to longevity.

28. On the day they are ordered out to battle, your soldiers may weep, those sitting up bedewing their garments, and those lying down letting the tears run down their cheeks. But let them once be brought to bay, and they will display the courage of a Chu or a Kuei.

29. The skillful tactician may be likened to the shuai-jan. Now the shuai-jan is a snake that is found in the ChUng mountains. Strike

at its head, and you will be attacked by its tail; strike at its tail, and you will be attacked by its head; strike at its middle, and you will be attacked by head and tail both.

30. Asked if an army can be made to imitate the shuai-jan, I should answer, Yes. For the men of Wu and the men of Yueh are enemies; yet if they are crossing a river in the same boat and are caught by a storm, they will come to each other's assistance just as the left hand helps the right.

31. Hence it is not enough to put one's trust in the tethering of horses, and the burying of chariot wheels in the ground

32. The principle on which to manage an army is to set up one standard of courage which all must reach.

33. How to make the best of both strong and weak—that is a question involving the proper use of ground.

34. Thus the skillful general conducts his army just as though he were leading a single man, willy-nilly, by the hand.

35. It is the business of a general to be quiet and thus ensure secrecy; upright and just, and thus maintain order.

36. He must be able to mystify his officers and men by false reports and appearances, and thus keep them in total ignorance.

37. By altering his arrangements and changing his plans, he keeps the enemy without definite knowledge. By shifting his camp and taking circuitous routes, he prevents the enemy from anticipating his purpose.

38. At the critical moment, the leader of an army acts like one who has climbed up a height and then kicks away the ladder behind him. He carries his men deep into hostile territory before he shows his hand.

39. He burns his boats and breaks his cooking-pots; like a shepherd driving a flock of sheep, he drives his men this way and that, and nothing knows whither he is going.

40. To muster his host and bring it into danger:—this may be termed the business of the general.

41. The different measures suited to the nine varieties of ground; the expediency of aggressive or defensive tactics; and the fundamental laws of human nature: these are things that must most certainly be studied.

42. When invading hostile territory, the general principle is, that penetrating deeply brings cohesion; penetrating but a short way means dispersion.

43. When you leave your own country behind, and take your army across neighborhood territory, you find yourself on critical ground. When there are means of communication on all four sides, the ground is one of intersecting highways.

44. When you penetrate deeply into a country, it is serious ground. When you penetrate but a little way, it is facile ground.

45. When you have the enemy's strongholds on your rear, and narrow passes in front, it is hemmed-in ground. When there is no place of refuge at all, it is desperate ground.

46. Therefore, on dispersive ground, I would inspire my men with unity of purpose. On facile ground, I would see that there is close connection between all parts of my army.

47. On contentious ground, I would hurry up my rear.

48. On open ground, I would keep a vigilant eye on my defenses. On ground of intersecting highways, I would consolidate my alliances.

49. On serious ground, I would try to ensure a continuous stream of supplies. On difficult ground, I would keep pushing on along the road.

50. On hemmed-in ground, I would block any way of retreat. On desperate ground, I would proclaim to my soldiers the hopelessness of saving their lives.

51. For it is the soldier's disposition to offer an obstinate resistance when surrounded, to fight hard when he cannot help himself, and to obey promptly when he has fallen into danger.

52. We cannot enter into alliance with neighboring princes until we are acquainted with their designs. We are not fit to lead an army on the march unless we are familiar with the face of the country—its mountains and forests, its pitfalls and precipices, its marshes and swamps. We shall be unable to turn natural advantages to account unless we make use of local guides.

53. To be ignored of any one of the following four or five principles does not befit a warlike prince.

54. When a warlike prince attacks a powerful state, his generalship shows itself in preventing the concentration of the enemy's forces. He overawes his opponents, and their allies are prevented from joining against him.

55. Hence he does not strive to ally himself with all and sundry, nor does he foster the power of other states. He carries out his own secret designs, keeping his antagonists in awe. Thus he is able to capture their cities and overthrow their kingdoms.

56. Bestow rewards without regard to rule, issue orders without regard to previous arrangements; and you will be able to handle a whole army as though you had to do with but a single man.

57. Confront your soldiers with the deed itself; never let them know your design. When the outlook is bright, bring it before their eyes; but tell them nothing when the situation is gloomy.

58. Place your army in deadly peril, and it will survive; plunge it into desperate straits, and it will come off in safety.

59. For it is precisely when a force has fallen into harm's way that is capable of striking a blow for victory.

60. Success in warfare is gained by carefully accommodating ourselves to the enemy's purpose.

61. By persistently hanging on the enemy's flank, we shall succeed in the long run in killing the commander-in-chief.

62. This is called ability to accomplish a thing by sheer cunning.

63. On the day that you take up your command, block the frontier passes, destroy the official tallies, and stop the passage of all emissaries.

64. Be stern in the council-chamber, so that you may control the situation.

65. If the enemy leaves a door open, you must rush in.

66. Forestall your opponent by seizing what he holds dear, and subtly contrive to time his arrival on the ground.

67. Walk in the path defined by rule, and accommodate yourself to the enemy until you can fight a decisive battle.

68. At first, then, exhibit the coyness of a maiden, until the enemy gives you an opening; afterwards emulate the rapidity of a running hare, and it will be too late for the enemy to oppose you.

XII.   THE ATTACK BY FIRE

1. Sun Tzu said: There are five ways of attacking with fire. The first is to burn soldiers in their camp; the second is to burn stores; the third is to burn baggage trains; the fourth is to burn arsenals and magazines; the fifth is to hurl dropping fire amongst the enemy.

2. In order to carry out an attack, we must have means available. The material for raising fire should always be kept in readiness.

3. There is a proper season for making attacks with fire, and special days for starting a conflagration.

4. The proper season is when the weather is very dry; the special days are those when the moon is in the constellations of the Sieve, the Wall, the Wing or the Cross-bar; for these four are all days of rising wind.

5. In attacking with fire, one should be prepared to meet five possible developments:

6. (1) When fire breaks out inside to enemy's camp, respond at once with an attack from without.

7. (2) If there is an outbreak of fire, but the enemy's soldiers remain quiet, bide your time and do not attack.

8. (3) When the force of the flames has reached its height, follow it up with an attack, if that is practicable; if not, stay where you are.

9. (4) If it is possible to make an assault with fire from without, do not wait for it to break out within, but deliver your attack at a favorable moment.

10. (5) When you start a fire, be to windward of it. Do not attack from the leeward.

11. A wind that rises in the daytime lasts long, but a night breeze soon falls.

12. In every army, the five developments connected with fire must be known, the movements of the stars calculated, and a watch kept for the proper days.

13. Hence those who use fire as an aid to the attack show intelligence; those who use water as an aid to the attack gain an accession of strength.

14. By means of water, an enemy may be intercepted, but not robbed of all his belongings.

15. Unhappy is the fate of one who tries to win his battles and succeed in his attacks without cultivating the spirit of enterprise; for the result is waste of time and general stagnation.

16. Hence the saying: The enlightened ruler lays his plans well ahead; the good general cultivates his resources.

17. Move not unless you see an advantage; use not your troops unless there is something to be gained; fight not unless the position is critical.

18. No ruler should put troops into the field merely to gratify his own spleen; no general should fight a battle simply out of pique.

19. If it is to your advantage, make a forward move; if not, stay where you are.

20. Anger may in time change to gladness; vexation may be succeeded by content.

21. But a kingdom that has once been destroyed can never come again into being; nor can the dead ever be brought back to life.

22. Hence the enlightened ruler is heedful, and the good general full of caution. This is the way to keep a country at peace and an army intact.

XIII. THE USE OF SPIES

1. Sun Tzu said: Raising a host of a hundred thousand men and marching them great distances entails heavy loss on the people and a drain on the resources of the State. The daily expenditure will amount to a thousand ounces of silver. There will be commotion at home and abroad, and men will drop down exhausted on the highways. As many as seven hundred thousand families will be impeded in their labor.

2. Hostile armies may face each other for years, striving for the victory which is decided in a single day. This being so, to remain in ignorance of the enemy's condition simply because one grudges the outlay of a hundred ounces of silver in honors and emoluments, is the height of inhumanity.

3. One who acts thus is no leader of men, no present help to his sovereign, no master of victory.

4. Thus, what enables the wise sovereign and the good general to strike and conquer, and achieve things beyond the reach of ordinary men, is foreknowledge.

5. Now this foreknowledge cannot be elicited from spirits; it cannot be obtained inductively from experience, nor by any deductive calculation.

6. Knowledge of the enemy's dispositions can only be obtained from other men.

7. Hence the use of spies, of whom there are five classes: (1) Local spies; (2) inward spies; (3) converted spies; (4) doomed spies; (5) surviving spies.

8. When these five kinds of spy are all at work, none can discover the secret system. This is called "divine manipulation of the threads." It is the sovereign's most precious faculty.

9. Having local spies means employing the services of the inhabitants of a district.

10. Having inward spies, making use of officials of the enemy.

11. Having converted spies, getting hold of the enemy's spies and using them for our own purposes.

12. Having doomed spies, doing certain things openly for purposes of deception, and allowing our spies to know of them and report them to the enemy.

13. Surviving spies, finally, are those who bring back news from the enemy's camp.

14. Hence it is that which none in the whole army are more intimate relations to be maintained than with spies. None should be more liberally rewarded. In no other business should greater secrecy be preserved.

15. Spies cannot be usefully employed without a certain intuitive sagacity.

16. They cannot be properly managed without benevolence and straightforwardness.

17. Without subtle ingenuity of mind, one cannot make certain of the truth of their reports.

18. Be subtle! be subtle! and use your spies for every kind of business.

19. If a secret piece of news is divulged by a spy before the time is ripe, he must be put to death together with the man to whom the secret was told.

20. Whether the object be to crush an army, to storm a city, or to assassinate an individual, it is always necessary to begin by finding out the names of the attendants, the aides-de-camp, and door-keepers and sentries of the general in command. Our spies must be commissioned to ascertain these.

21. The enemy's spies who have come to spy on us must be sought out, tempted with bribes, led away and comfortably housed. Thus they will become converted spies and available for our service.

22. It is through the information brought by the converted spy that we are able to acquire and employ local and inward spies.

23. It is owing to his information, again, that we can cause the doomed spy to carry false tidings to the enemy.

24. Lastly, it is by his information that the surviving spy can be used on appointed occasions.

25. The end and aim of spying in all its five varieties is knowledge of the enemy; and this knowledge can only be derived, in the first instance, from the converted spy. Hence it is essential that the converted spy be treated with the utmost liberality.

26. Of old, the rise of the Yin dynasty was due to I Chih who had served under the Hsia. Likewise, the rise of the Chou dynasty was due to Lu Ya who had served under the Yin.

27. Hence it is only the enlightened ruler and the wise general who will use the highest intelligence of the army for purposes of spying and thereby they achieve great results. Spies are a most important element in water, because on them depends an army's ability to move.

REFERENCES

BOOKS

Alexander, B. (2011) Sun Tzu at Gettysburg, New York: Norton

Anderson, J (1999) The Newhall Incident, Fresno: Quill Driver

Asken, M (2010) Warrior Mindset, USA: Warrior Science

Cantrell. R (2003) Understanding Sun Tzu on the Art of War, Arlington: Center for Advantage

Cullen, D (2009) Columbine, New York: Hachette Book Group

Doss, W (2003) Train to Win, USA: 1st Books

Gilmartin, K (2002) Emotional Survival for Law Enforcement, Tucson: E-S Press

Gladwell, M (2005) Blink, New York: Back Bay Books

Griffth, S (1963) Sun Tzu The Art of War: London: Oxford Press

Grossman / Christenson (2004) On Combat, USA: PPCT Research

Grossman, D (1995) On Killing, New York: Back Bay Books

Murray, K (2004) Training at the Speed of Life, Gotha: Armiger

Penrose, J (2004) D-Day, United Kingdom: Osprey Publishing

Plaster, J (2008) The History of Sniping and Sharpshooting, Boulder: Paladin Press

Siddle, B (1995) Sharpening the Warriors Edge, Belleville: PPCT Research

Thompson, G (2013) Verbal Judo - The Gentle Art of Persuasion, New York: Morrow

ARTICLES

Albrecht, S. "Contact and Cover," *Law Officer* (April 2007) pp 38-41

Dickinson, E. "The McDonald's Massacre" *Law Officer Magazine* (Aug 2013) pp 48-52

Freeman, T. "The Evolution of the Law Enforcement's Code of Ethics" *Law and Order* (Feb 1992) pp 63-66

Fretz, R. "An Officer's Firsthand Account of the Utah Mall Shooting Spree" *The Police Marksman* (March/April 2007) pp 46-47

Kulbarsh, P. "Police Suicide Rates in 2016" Officer.com (Jan 2017)

Labaj, L. "The Carver Methodology" *Journal of Counter-terrorism and Homeland Security International* (Vol. 17, No. 4) pp 42-46

Lesce, T. "The Rich History of SWAT" *Law and Order* (Apr 1996) pp 83-89

McKenna, B. "Officer Down, The Marcus Young Incident" *Law Officer* (June 2008) pp 44-49

Meyer, G. "40 Minutes in North Hollywood" *Police* (Jun 1997) pp 27-37

Papenfuhs, S. "Principle-Based Officer Safety Tactics" *The Police Marksman* (March/April 2003) pp 18-20

Young, M. "Good v Evil" *Law Officer Magazine* (Oct 2006) pp 38-47

VIDEO
"Surviving Edge Weapons" (1998) Caliber Press Video

STUDIES / REPORTS
Aamodt, M (2016) Law Enforcement Divorce Rates, Radford University

CA POST (2005) SWAT Operational Guidelines and Standardized Training, CA POST

FBI, Law Enforcement Officer Killed and Assaulted (LEOKA)

Los Angeles County Sheriff's Office (2010) Split Second Decisions, LASO

Stone, M (1994) The Rodney King Incident - The Gap Between Use of Force and Training

INDEX